T0346484

ORO Editions
Publishers of Architecture, Art, and Design
Gordon Goff: Publisher

www.oroeditions.com
info@oroeditions.com

Published by ORO Editions

Author: Franco Pisani
Foreword: Igor Marjanović
Afterword: Jonathan Foote
Book Design: Alicia Moreira
Project Coordinator: Alejandro Guzman-Avila
Managing Editor: Jake Anderson

10 9 8 7 6 5 4 3 2 1 First Edition

ISBN: 978-1-954081-16-1

Color Separations and Printing: ORO Group Ltd.
Printed in China.

ORO Editions makes a continuous effort to minimize the overall carbon footprint of its publications. As part of this goal, ORO Editions, in association with Global ReLeaf, arranges to plant trees to replace those used in the manufacturing of the paper produced for its books. Global ReLeaf is an international campaign run by American Forests, one of the world's oldest nonprofit conservation organizations. Global ReLeaf is American Forests' education and action program that helps individuals, organizations, agencies, and corporations improve the local and global environment by planting and caring for trees.

franco pisani

20x14.

reflections on
studying architecture
abroad.

ORO
EDITIONS

Table of Contents.

A.
Oceanic Feeling.
A Foreword by Igor Marjanović

Igor Marjanović is the JoAnne Stolaroff Cotsen Professor of Architecture and Chair of the Undergraduate Architecture Program at Washington University in St. Louis. Since 2007 he has been leading the Florence Summer Program, which was awarded the 2009 American Institute of Architects (AIA) Education Honor Award.

For Anna and Francesca, the main characters of Silvia Avallone's novel *Swimming to Elba*, the island could not have appeared more different than the port city of Piombino, in Tuscany, their rust-belt industrial hometown. Walking down Via Stalingrado, they arrive at the beach, rushing into the water, gazing at Elba in the distance. So close geographically, the island is nevertheless a world away from Piombino, a city marred by unemployment and poverty. Despite this separation, Anna and Francesca feel connected to both of these worlds by the deep blue sea, often daydreaming of swimming to the island. The water was a medium of both reflection and separation, and Anna in particular "loved the feel of that sea bottom, *rough and soft at the same time* ... underwater, where the noises of the world became a placenta, where the salt burns your corneas, where the only sound you can hear is your own breathing, no longer yours."[II]

In the distance, two and a half miles across the water, the white beaches of the Isle of Elba gleamed like an unattainable paradise. The inviolate domain of the Milanese, the Germans, the silky-skinned tourists in black SUVs and sunglasses. But for the teenagers who lived in the huge barracks of public housing, for the children of all the nobodies dripping with sweat and blood at the steel mill, the beach across the way from their front doors was already paradise. The only real paradise.[I]

–Silvia Avallone

[I] Epigraph: Silvia Avallone, *Swimming to Elba*, trans. Antony Shugaar (New York: Viking/Penguin, 2012), 10.

[II] Avallone, *Swimming to Elba*, 75 (emphasis mine).

Avallone's depiction has a particular personal meaning for me: in 2011 I too was struck by the contrast between the verdant island of Elba and Piombino's endless smokestacks. As my friend Franco and I drove through the city, we experienced firsthand some of the sights and smells that captivated Anna and Francesca so much: that strange ambience of both natural beauty and industrial pollution. In the decade that followed, we spent many hours talking about such idiosyncrasies. We swam together on Elba, looking at Piombino's smokestacks and Elba's abandoned mines, all while gazing at the Tuscan archipelago and counting the islands and islets that tourists saw as resorts but that we loved for their infrastructure of tunnels and mines.

Our conversations have been ongoing ever since—on the Vespas and ferries, in the cars and buses, in the streets and piazzas, over many meals or coffees. They allowed me to engage Italian culture and reconcile its numerous binary opposites: coastal and mountainous, industrial and picturesque, northern and southern. In many ways traveling is a conversation—with oneself and one's own culture but also with others and other cultures—so consequently this book is a conversation too. It is a snapshot of experiences that can—perhaps better than any textbook or orientation session—prepare a student for that ultimate conversation that we call studying abroad. It is a dialogue that is both enchanting and unsettling. Consequently, there is a conjuring "roughness" and "softness" in the book that you are about to read and that I am delighted to introduce. It is particularly important for American readers to embrace Franco's wit and honesty most directly, so they can see themselves not as soldiers of the world's greatest empire but as humble learners willing to embrace another culture and to look differently at their own.

I founded the Florence Summer Program in 2007 as a series of studios titled *Disegno: Encounters in Public Space*, referencing the origins of the English word *design* in the medieval Florentine word *disegno*—meaning both the drawing of a line on paper and the mental projection of an idea. Engaging global mobility, immigration, and diaspora, the program maps the stories of "locals" and "foreigners"—in particular the routes of illegal immigrants and refugees at sea, on the land, and in public spaces—allowing the students to develop a sense of knowledge and empathy that illuminates not only their time in Italy but also their design work in the United States. In the process, the students not only embrace the *other* but ultimately start to think of themselves as *others* too, boldly embracing multiple identities in a rapidly changing world.

This book erases distinctions between locals and foreigners and instead proposes a warm bond between the two. This is important, because none of us are strangers to multiple identities—in particular as we migrate and travel around the world. I still remember a distinct unease when my new Italian friends tried to connect me with the rest of the so-called expat community. This was a completely new term for me. While I have lived in many places around the world—Brazil, Russia, Serbia, the United States, and now even Italy—I was always an immigrant, an Eastern European coming from the "other" side of the Adriatic Sea. In Italy, Slavic people like myself were known as *Schiavoni*, laborers and serfs, whose traces still exist in the names of streets and paintings in Venice (or *Mleci* as it is known in Serbo-Croatian). Indeed the word *slave* in both English and Italian comes from the word Slavic—a big distinction from the "expats" who were considered to be mostly (wealthy) "Westerners" or exiles by choice. Having grown up in Belgrade and arrived in Florence from my "adopted" hometown of St. Louis, Missouri, I thus possessed a strange mix of backgrounds: I was both an immigrant and an expat, also benefiting from the wealth and privilege that comes from teaching at one of America's greatest universities.

My conversations with Franco blossomed around these manifold forms of citizenship—we were "expats" and "immigrants" all at once, American and Serbian, Italian and global, architects and teachers, soccer fans and lovers of art. We both enjoyed these multiple identities, musing at the imperfections of my flawed Italian and his much better English. We shared in the joy of the world as it was, all too often enjoying a plate of intestine stew made by Lorenzo and his sons in the gritty suburb of Novoli (which reminded me so much of my mother's Serbian cooking). Through these encounters we learned about each other's cultures, never losing sight that architecture begins not in a building's foundations but in the culture of a people—their laughter in times of happiness and their sorrow in times of tragedy. And the year 2020 was an extended time of pause as the world grappled with the global coronavirus pandemic. As we mourn the people whom we lost, we emerge stronger, for we know now more than ever what matters the most: the joys and mishaps of cultural exchange.

This book is a two-way street: it is a stream of consciousness of a teacher who has introduced many students to Italy but also a record of his own learning from the students. Earlier this year Franco called me in the aftermath of Breonna Taylor's murder, and we talked for a long time. A student of his had recommended Maya Angelou's book *I Know Why the Caged Bird Sings*, and when he discovered that a part of the book is set in her (and my) hometown of St. Louis, we talked about the impact of racism on people and buildings. This conversation is just one of many examples of how our conversations intensified even though we could not meet in person or go to Elba. Instead of the Mediterranean Sea, our phones became our oceans of connectivity, and we continued our cross-cultural dialogue regardless, albeit with a renewed sense of political urgency. This experience of togetherness was perhaps not unlike Sigmund Freud's definition of "oceanic feeling"—a profound sense of belonging to "something limitless, unbounded." A source of religious sentiments in Freud's view, this was "a feeling of an indissoluble bond, of being one with the external world as a whole."[III] I have always understood "oceanic feeling" to be an even broader concept: a

III Sigmund Freud, *Civilization and Its Discontents*, trans. James Strachey (New York: Norton, 1962), 11–12.

bond connecting people to people, people to ideas, and people to the world, a bond that sews together our differences, binary opposites, and multiple identities—indeed, all the matter from which our wonderfully diverse world is made.

In stitching together various conversations and cultural perspectives, this book is "oceanic" too. It builds bridges among cultures, reinforcing a sense of belonging to the larger world and making the case for the continued importance of international encounters. It is a poetic reminder that viruses and politicians will come and go but that travel and study abroad will prevail. No matter what, "we cannot fall out of this world—we are in it once and for all."[IV]

[IV] Christian Dietrich Grabbe, *Hannibal*, quoted in Freud, *Civilization and Its Discontents*, 12.

a mamma e babbo

00.

Introibo.

What a great start! Jumping in the midst of the scene, without preliminaries or too many formalities, with a measured sense of irony, which gives the scene lightness and speed, almost like a movie script. It's a perfect way to break the ice and get started. But (alas) I'm not James Joyce. So, it's a bit harder for me to introduce the reasons and the goal of this book. Nevertheless, let's give it a try!

Stately, plump Buck Mulligan came from the stairhead, bearing a bowl of lather on which a mirror and a razor lay crossed. A yellow dressing gown, ungirdled, was sustained gently-behind him by the mild morning air. He held the bowl aloft and intoned: - Introibo[00] ad altare Dei.

–James Joyce, Ulysses

Why 20?

I started to put together this book in the summer of 2020 (one of the weirdest summers of the last century), when I realized that—for the first time in 20 years—I was not going to have a new group of students to meet at the end of August, a site and a topic to choose, and a series of lectures to re-organize. It's not my habit to complain and I don't like students who complain "professionally." So, I decided to invest my unexpectedly free time on Mondays and Wednesdays (when I wouldn't be teaching architecture classes) in some sort of document condensing all I taught to and learned from my former students.

[00] Introibo: In Latin is the first person, future tense of the verb "*introīre*" to enter. It is the first word of the Latin verse *introibo ad altare Dei* ("I will go up to the altar of God") of Psalm 42 which, before the Vatican Second Ecumenical Council, the priest pronounced below the altar at the beginning of the mass.

Why 14?

Because 14 weeks is the length of a usual regular semester abroad: fourteen weeks, Monday through Thursday (Fridays are usually left free for site visits and to organize weekend trips), plus a one-week break in the middle to travel and experience Europe. Fall and Spring are regular semesters, the first starting in the last week of August and ending in the first week of December; the second starting in January and ending in late April or early May.

Both semesters have something remarkable and unique to offer; so, it's hard to pick one. In the fall, students arrive in shorts and go away when Christmas decorations have already been set up in the streets. Fall semester enrollees can visit the Biennale exhibition in Venice and enjoy the foliage season. True enough, Italy is not Vermont; yet, the way nature changes its colors in October can be impressive here too.

In the spring, students arrive with sunset around 5 p.m. By the end of the semester, daylight saving time has been back for a while already and the days are long and almost always sunny. The city changes less in colors and attitudes, but halfway through the semester the coming of spring is energizing (despite the higher risk of rainy weather).

Why 20x14?

I chose this title because I like cycling. In fact, I'm obsessed with bicycles (one of the best inventions ever). In cycling slang, 20x14 (twenty by fourteen) sounds like a chainring and sprocket combination. A 20-tooth chainring is not very common, except in some old mountain bikes. Yet, if combined with a 14-tooth sprocket it would give a very short metric development, about 3 meters per pedal stroke, which would serve as an exceptional ally to tackle impossible climbs with high cadence, saving your legs from lactic acid.

I hope this "agile" title is a good omen to tackle the very hard climb that education abroad is called to face in the incoming months (without my legs hurting too much, if possible).

What is 20x14?
A vademecum? A to-do list? A series of recommendations? Something like the infamous 10 top things to do in Florence that you can find in many websites?

All of the above, but—to be honest—I chose this format to have a framework, a series of shelves (as it were) to organize the flow of my thoughts. After all, I'm not an English native speaker but an Italian architect instead. So, this format helped me find a rhythm, a good pace for the text. Formally, the book consists of a list of twenty suggestions (or paternal exhortations, if you will) which I've drawn from twenty years of teaching architecture students abroad. From a distance (in retrospect, one may say), all of these arguments started to intertwine and melt into each other, till they became a single, wider reflection.

Who is this book written for?

Is it just for architecture students abroad? Not necessarily; architecture students are the starting point, the "enzymes"—as it were—that triggered everything. I started teaching architecture students abroad by chance nearly twenty years ago in the fall of 2001. From this experience I think I have gained the knowledge and the critical distance necessary to have something relevant to share.

This said, I hope that the hints and the suggestions shared in this book can be useful to (and appreciated by) every student, from any major and any level of education. This also applies to those who wish to undertake an experience abroad, have already undertaken it or simply want to reflect on an experience that (although finished) is still very vivid in their memory.

Students only?

It depends on how we define the notion of being a student. If students are only those who pay tuition fees to a school, then these pages are not addressed to them only. But if students are all those people who are curious and still able to learn something from anything (either through an officially organized program or on their own), then this book is indeed for students.

The reflections that I want to share are a wider way of raising questions on the present, the possible future and the actual challenges of international education (not just for architecture programs) in this very peculiar age, where distances have been killed—at least apparently—by the Internet first and, more recently, by the protocols connected with the Covid pandemic.

Going back to James Joyce's quote, the book is addressed to all the curious and brave Ulysses that are still able to appreciate diversity and distance from home.

People have always traveled throughout the Italian peninsula. In ancient times, traders did it out of necessity. Then pilgrims began to go to Rome for indulgences. Lastly, artists and architects started to travel to Italy either looking for inspiration or trying to learn from foreign masters.

Between the eighteenth and nineteenth centuries, a trip to the *Bel paese*[01] became an almost compulsory step in the education of young people from wealthy European and American families, so as to complete traditional academic education with private tutors.

Until the last century, "tourism" (at least as we know it today) did not exist. The vast majority of people practically never left the city where they lived and worked, if not out of necessity.

In most cases, traveling was inaccessible, expensive, and not easy to undertake. But traveling abroad posited a further problem:

[01] Bel paese, literally translated as "the beautiful country", is one of the nicknames commonly given to Italy. We find it already in Dante «*il bel paese dove 'l sì suona*» (*Inferno*, Canto XXXIII) and in Petrarca «*il bel paese / ch'Appennin parte e 'l mar circonda e l'Alpe*» (*Canzoniere*, CXLVI).

language. Very few people knew a foreign language back then.

Nowadays, travellers reach Italy prompted by their desire for knowledge, by their wish for discovery, by their love for the history and the art of this country. In sum, Italy serves as a symbol of classicism, but also as a promise of a different relationship with time, values, nature, and landscape.

American universities started to offer study abroad options at the turn of the twenty-first century; the first official American program established in Firenze was Smith College in 1931. Nearly ninety years of semesters abroad have been hosted by this city. In the course of almost a century, the role of the semester abroad has changed a lot, especially in architecture. The traditional Grand Tour—i.e., the almost necessary step in architectural education (just think of the tour to Italy that Le Corbusier took in 1907 and Louis Khan in 1929)—has become quite different now that the world is electronically connected and all places and cultures are jumbled in a continuous time-place fusion, while—strangely enough—opposite tendencies are determining the rise of local cultures and the expression of place (dialects, identities, food, and costumes).

Between these two forces (something like expansion on the one hand and contraction on the other), a new meaning for study abroad is being defined. Big changes are introduced due to globalization and to the different perception of space that has been violently introduced by the terminal velocity of social media and their massive diffusion.

In this digitally virtual era, thanks to the smartphones that—everywhere and all the time—people hold in their hands, it is possible to brutalize physical distances and skip spatial barriers. A common idea of "citizens of the world" is being shaped, making people believe that they can move and adapt without limits and without any kind of emotional reaction, as if unease or nostalgia were obstacles to productivity and progress.

At first, this may sound like a perfect condition. In truth, though, it is precisely those levels of discomfort that make a semester abroad an incredibly valuable experience.

Unfortunately, students often decide to spend a semester abroad as if they were only ticking a box in a form, just like one of the countless options offered by educational institutions competing to attract as many students as possible. Among US students today, a semester abroad seems to have become a "must" mostly to boost one's own Instagram profile (rather than strengthening a serious academic CV). Being less motivated results in reduced awareness of what a twelve-hour flight means and may lead to, both geographically and anthropologically.

Today, more than ever, traveling abroad demands awareness about distances and constant efforts to understand contexts. Study abroad is a training pit to face the challenges launched by this new world, where we will often be nomads (sometimes by choice, sometimes by necessity, sometimes in business class, sometimes inside a shipping container).

For a semester, students abroad live in a peculiar condition: they are travelers as well as citizen apprentices, neither tourists nor hosts.

And this is the value of being abroad for an apprentice architect: from the detached but internal position of a student abroad, you can see more clearly the context without the emotional ties that being a citizen imposes on you.

On the one hand you feel the pleasure of discovering, on the other you feel regret for leaving home. One semester (fourteen weeks) is the perfect time span to represent more than a trip and less of a permanence.

An academic semester abroad in Italy means residing in a foreign country for no less than four months, with all that this implies. To put it bluntly, you study abroad not only for the monuments but also—and more importantly—for everything that stands between the monuments. In the streets and in the piazzas of an Italian city, confronted with what you will at first consider the odd ways the residents behave and their unknown language, you shall gradually find yourselves by paying attention to other peoples' lives. Away from the conventions of your previous, ordinary life and the ease of your language, a semester abroad becomes a sort of mirror, where you can spot your real self and your values.

This is also very true from the teacher's point of view. I've been intrigued by teaching foreign students, both here in "Firenze" and in their comfort zone in the USA. It's a precious opportunity to get to know new realities, but—more importantly—it is a great opportunity for me to see my habits and my comfort zone from a further perspective, so as to better understand how they work.

Even if camouflaged in normality, a semester abroad is a complex psychological experience for everyone. Inevitably, it entails moments of crisis, as it forces a radical reorganization of daily routines, thus influencing (to various extents) one's sense of identity. While abroad, the ties with significant people, their things, their language, their climate and habits are lost; as a consequence, a strong feeling of estrangement towards the new living environment (especially early on in the semester) can take over.

This situation is generally known as "Ulysses Syndrome" or the emigrant syndrome. Sometimes it leads travellers to idealize their native country, where everything appears to be beautiful, even idyllic, and— more importantly—accessible. Meanwhile, people affected by this syndrome devalue the country of arrival, seeing it as a cause of hardship, embarrassment or suffering.

Yet, the exact opposite can also occur, that is, over evaluating the host country as a constantly funny and pleasant promised land, in contrast to one's own country, which starts to be seen as the cause of all evils.

Let's briefly go back to the first page of James Joyce's *Ulysses,* which I quoted at the beginning of this chapter for both narrative and stylistic reasons. That Ulysses (whose "real" name is Leopold Bloom) is different from Homer's Ulysses in the *Odyssey* (after whom the syndrome is named). And yet, the plot of those two stories and the reflections triggered by their experiences are related.

For starters, both characters symbolize the adventurous and—to a certain extent—epic trip (although one lasting ten years, the other just one day) of a human being in this world. Both protagonists build their own identity while traveling and facing different random events and difficulties.

Also, they both enrich themselves through the diversity they encounter, managing not to be either physically destroyed or psychologically absorbed. In both stories, the boundary between "inside" and "outside" becomes feeble, and the physicality of the events interbreed itself with the inner flow of the characters' thoughts, thus transforming what would otherwise be simply ordinary and random into special opportunities for growth.

The very same thing can happen during your semester abroad, provided this experience is approached with the right attitude, thus letting the "outside" influence your "inside" and vice versa.

Please, make the plot of your own four-month-long voyage as relevant for your identity as those narrated by Homer and Joyce.

It only depends on you.

01.

Don't be shy! Put some more ...

You are abroad!

Even if it looks like everyone speaks understandable Internet English, you are in a foreign country. More than 4,000 miles from your so-called comfort zone.

There is nothing you must be ashamed of, if you don't get something. Each time something is not clear, ask about it or at least take some notes about it on your sketchbook and ask for (or about) it later. Don't try to avoid misunderstandings by skipping the situation or the argument. Each question is a good opportunity to enrich yourself, and to make your semester abroad more valuable. The question is more important than the answer. In fact, the question is not only a request for some missing information, but an opportunity to force yourself to think and argue about something that—for some reason (and not by chance)—is obscure to you. And this second option often turns out to be more important than the answer your teacher might give you.

Be patient toward all that is unsolved in your heart and to try to love the questions themselves like locked rooms and like books that are written in a very foreign tongue. Do not now seek the answers, which cannot be given you because you would not be able to live them. And the point is, to live everything. Live the questions now. Perhaps you will then gradually, without noticing it, live along some distant day into the answer.
–Rainer Maria Rilke

If you are shy, relax! Of course, I'm not speaking of your deep, psychological profile. I respect that more than you can imagine, because I've been a shy student myself. I'm speaking of the stereotyped approach students have when they prefer not to ask questions for fear of being judged. More precisely, I'm speaking of your presence in a new city and particularly in a new studio environment during your semester abroad. So, don't be shy. There are at least two sound reasons for this. First: time abroad goes by faster than at home. Second: while abroad you can learn that earning grades is not the main reason for you to attend classes.

Time (not the grade) is our currency. Spend it wisely, especially while abroad.

The first week, during orientation, it seems there is plenty of time ahead of you, nearly four months, fifteen weekends to be filled with travels and amazing adventures. However, final presentations day will be here before you know it. And packing will start immediately after. In other words, don't waste time on meaningless hesitations or excuses (they are for losers); in doing so, you are tricking yourself not your teachers. In a nutshell: don't schedule for next week things that can be done today.

More importantly, make every day special. Even if social media and on-line apps can give us the illusion of being at home wherever we are, in fact you are very far from home and it won't happen to you every day to be on this side of "the pond."

I beg you to believe what I'm about to say and keep it in mind: even the oddest things, although overlooked at first, will start looking familiar very soon. In Firenze, Roma o Venezia—or any other city where you may be studying abroad—it is really sad to think that one can get used to some kind of context to the point of not being able to realize it anymore. In his *Diario Fiorentino*, the German poet Rainer Maria Rilke (who spent a couple of weeks in Firenze in 1898) warns his readers as follows: "[Don't become] like that guy who lived next to Schubert or Beethoven: at first the uninterrupted flow of music disturbed him, then irritated him and in the end he didn't even hear that music anymore."[02]

[02] Rainer Maria Rilke, *Diaries of a Young Poet* (New York: W.W. Norton & Co., 1997), 76.

Often our hesitation is simply a way of defending ourselves against something we perceive as uncomfortable. To be honest, I must admit that—although some incredibly brilliant teachers (humility is the mother of all virtues …) may become your guides when you study abroad—the best learning outcomes will be triggered by moments of discomfort and odd questions.

This will only be possible if you keep your attention level high. Living in a place that is apparently impossible to decipher is the core of being abroad. Learning to buy bread or ask for a drink, understanding why clothes are hanging shamelessly outside the windows. This is tantamount to transforming your daily life into memorable lessons.

I thus urge you to follow lectures and desk crits actively. This implies asking questions when things are not clear. Discussions on topic are always welcome. Don't be afraid of spending more than three words to express your feelings.

A desk crit is not a confession, and designs are not secret products of your inviolable and intimate creativity. Teamwork is a precious opportunity to learn to share ideas and compare points of view.

If you are shy because you don't want to be judged for your questions, be shy also when you do stupid things like falling asleep in class or skipping studio after your desk crit. This behaviour reveals who you are more than your questions do, trust me. In studio, when you don't help facing a problem you are part of it.

Don't be afraid of the grading policy adopted by your teacher while abroad; be afraid of banality and of stupidity, instead, and stay away from them.

Do studio stuff for yourselves, not for the grade.

Abroad, some studios release credits, some don't. Some studios have grades, some only p/f policy.

Abroad, you can learn to be less afraid of grades. A third year's student of architecture must be aware of the fact that the most important thing from this year on is the portfolio.

I never heard of people who didn't get a job because of their GPA, but I could mention a lot of former students who have been hired thanks to the engaging, original portfolios they developed while studying abroad. In the course of a semester abroad you can develop those pages that I usually call "hook pages", that is, pages that can make the reader stop while browsing the portfolio and re-address the conversation.

Come on, don't be shy: put some more (work into your portfolio)!

02.

You are a student abroad, not a tourist!

Under Italian law, to get the status of "student abroad" you are asked to produce appropriate documentation, an International Health Insurance (specifically issued for your trip to Italy) for urgent medical care and hospitalisation, and—*conditio sine qua non*—a certificate attesting your enrollment at an Italian institution, with proof of full payment of the selected courses, the number of hours of lesson attended each month, and the starting and ending dates of the academic program.

These certificates are expected to prove your legal status. However, they will prove nothing as far as your attitude toward education is concerned.

In my opinion, the only condition that can give you the attitude of a student (no matter your age, gender, health condition and, more importantly if you are enrolled in a program or on your own) is your ability for learning.

You are a student if you learn something; other than that, you are a tourist.

Is it possible to impose learning, to force someone to assimilate knowledge as if it were like taking a medicine? No. Likewise, it is impossible to learn by simply sitting at lectures or at your desk in studio.

Learning only happens if you want it to happen and if you make it happen.

The verb "to learn" comes from Old English *leornian* ("to get knowledge, be cultivated; study, read, think about"), which in turn derives from Proto-Germanic *lisnojanan* ("to follow" or "to find a track"). As I'm sure you have noticed, all of these actions demand will and commitment.

Also from a grammatical point of view, to learn is a transitive verb. As such, it requires a subject and an object; the action moves from an "agent" to a "patient."

Differently than what most people believe, the verb to learn is an active verb because it must have an agent, someone or something producing a phenomenon. It takes will and determination to be an agent. If you are eager to learn, all of the things you discover on your own (out of commitment and perseverance or even by stumbling upon them, reproducing them, making mistakes and trying again), will make a deeper mark on your education than anything you may be forced to study.

You must be determined to learn; learning doesn't happen by chance as encounters do. For learning to happen, you must intentionally leave your doors wide open. And this is another skill your experience abroad can improve a lot.

Like any other discipline, learning architecture is a practice that must lead us to generously open our doors so as to learn from whatever surrounds us, merging ourselves in an active way in this constantly changing world, as a seed in fertile ground. Learning sprouts, as seeds do, only in favorable conditions. **You can't force seeds to sprout, but you can try to create the conditions (the good ground) for them to sprout.**

Abroad, if you want, this can be an easier task, because everything looks new and unknown.

You must wake up everyday thinking: "I'm abroad. Today I want to learn something!"

Architecture—as any form of art—is hard to define with words and to convey in a brief, scientific, exact formula. It requires dedication more than talent. In architecture, learning never ends; basically, one continues to be a student even after graduation. For this reason, schools of architecture are open labs, where learning and teaching are continuously, inevitably intertwined.

Studio attendance is usually mandatory. Yet, attendance is not enough to learn architecture.

Although necessary, attending lectures, meeting with the professor during office hours or actively participating in crits and pin-ups are only a small part of your job. You must commit yourself with determination and a spirit of sacrifice.

By designing, a synthesis between technical-scientific knowledge on the one hand and humanistic culture on the other is achieved. Simply put, all artefacts (from the humblest tool to the most sophisticated system) are conceived, designed, and produced by human beings for other human beings.

In architecture one learns design by designing with and for others, be they friends, teachers, peers or strangers.

Nowadays we can say that learning to design no longer consists in the absorption of a set of immutable rules and codes, but in adopting an open sensitivity to the world. There is no better place to train this sensitivity than abroad.

By drawing physical models or descriptions, shaping a vision through design should be a vital need for an architect, at once challenging and highly engaging and yet as natural as breathing or sleeping.

If you've never felt this urge, and you consider your project only a boring academic assignment, I believe you should honestly ask yourself if architecture is the right major for you.

Bored people are more dangerous than we can imagine.

The built environment is already suffering from lack of vision and good design. Future architects must be seen as a potential cure to these pathologies, not as one of their causes.

Schools of architecture are training fields for such a responsibility, both at home and—even more importantly—when one is abroad.

03.

Work hard, play safe!

Don't be intimidated by work. Something my mother taught me is that hard work and commitment always pay off; "maybe not every Friday," she used to say, "but sooner or later they always do."

Design is an iterative and fertile process, with plenty of bifurcations. Try to finalize your ideas on different media and using different tools, sketches, drawings, watercolors, models, pictures, tales, movies and more Ideas need to be cultivated, fed, verified, supported, and helped. Don't wait for your teachers' approval; produce as much as you can.

And it is most true that all work done with pleasure and worthy of praise produces art, that is to say an essential part of the pleasure of life.

–William Morris, *Art and Labour*

"I'm confused, I got stuck because I don't know what to do. I didn't understand what you expect from me ..." This is what most students say at desk crits when they don't have any drawings to discuss or they didn't do their work.

Students often come to desk crits with a small sketch that they have put together just twenty minutes before and then they spend a lot of words commenting on it. How can you pretend that a desk crit lasts longer than the time you invested to produce and lay out your ideas?

Don't be afraid of getting tired or bored by designing. If that happens, pay attention: it could be the symptom of a more serious malaise.

"What am I supposed to do for Monday? First plans or cross sections? Models must be produced as a first or last deliverable?"

There are no rules about the evolution and the improvement of a project. The only rule is that a project won't evolve by itself; it needs hard work and many attempts. An architecture project must be carried out thoroughly, in three dimensions, using all the methods and media available. Computer software is just a tool to develop projects, like all the other more traditional tools. Usually, desk crits turn out better if made on paper than on screen. Nevertheless, in studio we must use all the available tools. Besides, it's difficult to help you arrange things on a screen right away (especially if a language barrier gets in the way).

Bring everything with you during desk crits; we will work on things done, not on intentions.

Start working as soon as possible, on a daily basis and with continuity; don't wait till the last week to become productive. A few hours a day produce better results than a series of sleepless nights by the end of the semester. When you are happy with what you have done, take a rest. A field that has rested gives a bountiful crop. As Ovid said: *"Continua messe senescit ager"* [03] (A field becomes exhausted by constant tillage).

[03] Ovid, Ars Amatoria (London: Modern Library Edition, 2002),III,82.

Leave your drawings on your desk, but bring your vision home with you after Studio. Every moment is good for a twist to your project if you keep your brain connected: ideas also come when you are not looking for them.

With this mindset, while abroad you can learn that artists (that is, people involved in creativity) work also while doing their grocery shopping, walking home or even enjoying a nice drink before dinner. That's the kind of drink we Italians call *aperitivo* (from Latin "*aperitivus*", an "opening," like French *entrée*—"to enter"—referring to the small course before the main course): a drink meant to stimulate and, therefore, "open"/"pave" the way for appetite.

Don't feel blessed if your teachers abroad are not demanding; pretend a lot from them, instead. You may think that Studio abroad seems easier because your tutor is not pretending the same amount of deliverables you are used to producing at your home institution. True enough, by the end of your semester abroad you will probably get your passing grade in the box. But while abroad you are exposed to thousands of learning opportunities, if you want. You have free weekends to visit cities, to explore Europe, and to store up life experiences; but you also have four days a week to work on your architecture projects. Use the studio hours of your semester abroad to experience a different way of producing by valuing "quality" over "quantity." Try to focus more on how you work than on how much you work. **Ideas are not evaluated by weight.**

An amazing project doesn't need hundreds of drawings. An astonishing drawing (one layered in time and space, correct and finely crafted) is better than an infinite set of tasteless, unfinished drawings that anyone can pull off by simply following the syllabus checklist.

04.

Read and look at the pictures! Carefully.

I'm fascinated by (and a bit obsessed with) books. If I walk into a bookstore, I can't resist and I end up buying something. Yet, I must confess that I haven't read all the books I own, although I know exactly on which shelf most of them "live."

This said, I must add that googling is not reading. With their lack of visual support, books stand out to me as a great training routine for the brain and a valuable fuel for imagination. This is not a nostalgic suggestion; I don't see reading as an old school practice. Reading (books, drawings or spaces) and writing (with letters, lines or walls) are two opposite ways of exchanging values, representing intake (the former) and output (the latter). In both cases, it's an important exercise in translation from the ideal to the material, from the abstract to the concrete and backward, the like of which cannot be found in other methods. Architecture is an indissoluble mix of ideality and materiality. As the

El verbo leer, como el verbo amar y el verbo soñar, no soporta 'el modo imperativo.' Yo siempre les aconsejé a mis estudiantes que si un libro los aburre lo dejen; que no lo lean porque es famoso, que no lean un libro porque es moderno, que no lean un libro porque es antiguo. La lectura debe ser una de las formas de la felicidad y no se puede obligar a nadie a ser feliz.[04]

–Jorge Luis Borges

[04] The verb to read, like the verb to love and the verb to dream, doesn't bear the imperative mode. I always advised my students to drop reading a book when it starts to be uninteresting. They don't have to read it because it's famous, they don't have to read it because it's modern, or antique. Reading should be one of the ways to happiness and nobody can be forced to be happy. (Trans. by the Author)

ancient Roman architect Vitruvius put it: *Ea nascitur ex fabrica et ratiocinatione* ("It is born of doing and thinking").

Architects must be intellectuals who feed—at once—the brain and the body.

On a semester abroad, every single day students are forced to transfer information between two different lifestyles. This constant dynamic can lead them to discover (or rediscover) the hidden pleasure of the slow pace of reading.

They can do so by following in the footsteps of great writers who felt the need of stopping some magic moments of their experience abroad. For instance, they may go through the six experiences suggested by John Ruskin's *Mornings in Florence* or chasing Rainer Maria Rilke's *Florentine Diary*.

Among other institutions, Firenze hosts the National Library of Italy. It's an immense repository of knowledge (free and accessible) with an amazing, huge reading room full of students.

Like artefacts, books—even when written in an unknown and unreadable language—are incredibly inspiring for an architect.

Luckily enough, architecture books are often precious objects full of visuals of all kinds: intriguing graphics, beautiful pictures, and nicely drafted drawings, which make books apparently more accessible. But be careful: the traditional reminder "Don't just look at the pictures!" is not always valid for architects, especially those traveling abroad. Drawings and pictures are readable, just like texts, if not more. They shouldn't be seen as a decoration to reduce the pressure of textual information and to make books more appealing. They are not sweeteners to make bitter drinks (as textbooks are often considered) more palatable. We must develop a capacity of studying visually pictures and drawings, to draw by heart the plan of Hadrian's Villa or of the Terragni's Danteum as we can repeat the rhymes of an immortal poetry.

Start to look at pictures with the curiosity of a detective, guessing in plan where the camera was placed to take that picture or where the glowing on the wall is coming from in the cross section. So an architect must look at the pictures and not simply see them, because they are mysterious codes of which we are not always able to understand the meaning but in which some intelligence could be sensed.

Is it possible to read a book that is written in an unknown language?

Is it possible to read a book that is not written with words and printed on paper or formatted on a PDF?

A student of architecture abroad has a mandatory reader even if it's not reported on any syllabus. Although not written in words, that text is still readable; it's the City.

The City is a textbook, compelling and surprising. To be understood it simply needs commitment and motivation, some vocabulary and grammar. And, last but not least, a good teacher to help you discover thoughts hidden behind shapes. The city and the opportunity to live in a city as a citizen is the main learning outcome for a semester abroad in architecture.

05 In Italy students are exempted from the "tassa di soggiorno." Also known as the tourist tax, it's a local tax applied to individuals using accommodation facilities in areas classified as tourist resorts or art cities.

The City is free and accessible, you don't have to pay an admission fee if you are a student abroad[05] or to swipe a badge to be able to get lost in it. The real classroom is outdoors; side school and studio must be the support to learn how to read the city.

If we look at the city from an etymological point of view, we discover something very important. The "city" (*la città* in Italian) owes its name to the citizens and not to its buildings. The word "*città*" (and, subsequently, the city) comes from Latin *civitas*, which was the venue where the community (the *cives*, i.e., the citizens) convened. So the word "city" comes from the word "citizen"; the city is a city because of its citizens and not the other way around (as most people think). The city is more about the content than about the container.

To study the city we must be able to see it as a living organism, always evolving together with the humans who live in it. Like all living organisms, the city changes in a seamless fashion; it's always the same but—at the same time—it's always different.

It's easier to notice how a person changes if we see him or her every once in a while, not every single day. The same is true of the city: changes happen as a feeble but unstoppable background noise. To spot changes you must tune yourself on their frequencies and be able to put things in perspective, introducing the variable of time and appreciating every single aspect of it (including uncomfortable ones). In sum, we must see monuments together with the fabric that connects them.

A city is the place where you can experience the unexpected, and learn to face it. In other words, the city is an educational tool.

A student abroad moves (often for the first time) from the relative security and predictability of the campus to the unpredictability of the city, where actions trigger (not always in a linear way) a series of reactions. In turn, reactions act like new actions, striking and affecting others. In today's world, people hardly go beyond what they know; in doing so, they lose an opportunity to become richer. Abroad you can learn to leave your pores wide open for the unknown, which—although scary—is where the most important things come from. It's— at once—where you come from and where you will go to. Being abroad is an opportunity to cultivate the art of getting lost.[06] To read the city is a difficult but necessary (and highly educative) task for a student of architecture. If conceived as a narrative, the city becomes readable, and it can tell stories. By reading this "book" we can learn two main things: the limits of unique authorship and the necessary unfinished nature of the human context. From this angle the city becomes both a living organism and the most important client an architect will serve (even if it won't pay your bills). When we design, we always contribute a verse to the choral book of the built environment of the city.

[06] Rebecca Solnit, *A Field Guide to Getting Lost* (New York: Penguin Group, 2006).

The city has been written (shaped, if you prefer) by life more than by codes and architects; it's a masterpiece that doesn't bear the signature of any single author. The city is a collaborative playlist where songs are connected by all kinds of associations; the more the associations are inspired, the more the playlist will work as a whole.

05.

BYOSB! (Bring your own sketchbook)

Literally translated, *Nulla dies sine linea* (the famous Latin proverbio Pliny the Elder's *Naturalis Historia* refers to) means "no day without a line."

Apelle fuit alioqui perpetua consuetudo: numquam tam occupatum diem agendi, ut non lineam ducendo exerceret, quod ab eo in proverbio veniit

–Pliny the Elder, *Naturalis Historia*

This phrase refers to the famous painter Apelles, who did not let a day go by without sketching some lines with the brush. In its common meaning, it wants to emphasize the need for daily exercise to achieve perfection and to make good progress.

For Apelles, no single day was so full of commitments to prevent him from exercising his drawing technique.

Do practice drawing as a daily discipline!

And use the semester abroad as an experiment to test your perseverance. Put down in your sketchbook everything you think is of some interest. This way, you won't lose it.

Get a sketchbook and keep it always with you: it will be the storage for thoughts, sketches, notes, ideas, and experiences: be curious and let your sketchbook be your diary!

Research is cumulative and prolific; every step is an opening towards unexpected views.

The first time I was asked to keep a sketchbook was for the interior design studio by professor Adolfo Natalini.

Arredamento e Architettura degli Interni has been traditionally the most prestigious teaching position at the School of Architecture in Firenze. For this reason, it has traditionally been held by some of the most important architects who taught there.

Professor Natalini used to ask students to keep a sketchbook by making at least one drawing a day. What subject? "Whatever!" he said. "What really matters is that you draw something everyday. One sketch a day; it doesn't have to be a beautiful one." At first, I thought that was a weird assignment. I must say, it took me some time to get started. The white pages of a brand new sketchbook can be very scary. But then I realized I was doing that only for myself, not for the professor or anyone else. It was just for me and for my own pleasure.

To make a long story short, I finished that sketchbook (which, by the way, the professor never checked) and—after that—I never stopped drawing. Since then, drawing has become a daily practice that I'm addicted to; it helps me to understand the world and it teaches me to express my ideas more clearly.

Contrary to what most people believe, drawing is a discipline that doesn't require rare skills or expensive tools; it only takes a lot of practice. And it is still one of the best training routines to keep the brain and the hands connected.

Usually students are afraid of drawing. Most of them are obsessed by the idea of a drawing as a masterpiece.

They think we draw to showcase.

But this is not true; as architects, we draw to think and to give shape to our ideas, to stop a vision.

As we become adults, we feel uncomfortable drawing. The reason is simple: most of us don't practice drawing anymore after we turn six or seven.

In Italy (like, I believe, in most—if not all—parts of the Western world) when six-year-old kids start going to school, they are pretty comfortable expressing themselves through visuals. They are not obsessed with the beauty or the photorealism of their sketches, nor are they ashamed of showing and explaining their drawings.

From September onwards in their first year of school, kids focus on learning how to read and write. By Christmas, almost all of them know how to write a simple letter to Santa Claus; it is at this point that the decline of their drawing skills starts.

Inexorably, our practice in sketching loses importance until—year after year—it is slowly abandoned.

I bet that, after we leave high school, most of us feel uncomfortable drawing!

Try to stop walking or reading for a couple of years and see what happens.

"My hands are shaking, my lines are not straight!" Well, start drawing five straight lines from A to B every morning when you have breakfast...Trust me: after only a couple of weeks, your lines will begin to look straight and elegant. Honestly, it takes much more time to learn to play tennis or to play the guitar.

When you are abroad for four months, you must change your habits, starting with basic, daily things: breakfast cereals are different in Italy and so is coffee; dinnertime is a couple of hours delayed. Briefly, everything is different.

So why don't you try to start practice drawing again?

Every morning, draw your coffee cup (not your walking mug, since nobody drinks coffee while walking in Italy); then move on to your "*cornetto*" or "*bombolone*" (two Italian kinds of pastries). Eventually, you will witness your skills magically starting to improve, day after day.

I remember that, when I was a university student, a professor gave a lecture on the Bialetti Moka coffee machine one day. Registered by Alfonso Bialetti in 1933, the Moka is an icon of Italian design but also one of the most common domestic objects in Italy. Everyone is familiar with it: we all see it, use it, and take care of it.

It was maybe my second year in the school of architecture. During a lesson in the Industrial Design course, I was surprised to see how the professor could speak for such a long time about something I was so used to.

The issue came when—after about 45 minutes of explanations and praise on what a great piece of design that was—the professor turned off the projector and asked us to draw it in plan, sections and elevation. "What a mess!"

While holding a pen, in front of a blank page, that object (which was so familiar to me until five minutes before) started to lose its shape, geometry, and details.

The image of that object—which until then I had considered so vivid in my brain—started to become foggy.

Was it eight sides or ten? Was the top part screwed into the bottom one or the other way around?

I felt terribly ashamed: I was not able to draw it with precision.

That day, after class, as soon as I got back home, I went to the kitchen, grabbed my own Moka coffee pot and started to redraw it carefully in my sketchbook. After those sketches, I never forgot it.

It goes without saying that the lesson learned was not only about the Moka; it was about drawing as a way to investigate and understand reality. Once you sketch something, you learn from it and what you have learned will remain with you forever.

Sketching takes time and commitment, much more time than a picture taken with our smartphone; this is what makes sketching both more selective and effective. Also, an on-site handmade drawing has more dimensions than a photo because of the vivid context it involves.

When I go back to the pages of some of my old sketchbooks I can feel exactly at what the temperature that sketch was created or I can clearly smell the same smells that were around me while sketching.

You may happen to be holding a Moka coffee pot in your hands right now. If you come to Italy for an academic semester abroad, I am pretty sure you will find one Moka coffee pot among the amenities in your apartment. In which case, don't treat it like a mysterious, alien object. Take it in your hands, observe it carefully, open it by unscrewing the top, remove the filter and study it with your eyes. Touch and sense the surface and the thickness of its various parts. Smell it. Then buy some ground coffee. When you do so, pay attention to its grain: the package must read *per Moka* not *per Espresso*. Once you have bought the right kind of coffee, use one of the tutorials you can easily find on the Internet and make yourself a nice cup of coffee. While sipping it, take your sketchbook and condense all your observations on a set of sketches.

Be careful: after making coffee, wash your Moka with water only. Never use dish soap on it, if you don't want your next coffee to taste like soap. Your sketches of Moka coffee machines will taste like coffee for the rest of your life, and the Moka will never look like an alien object to you again in your entire life.

And now, a few personal suggestions for your sketching routine: use ink pens of at least two line weights and never delete your drawings even when they are not nice. Change page, instead, and start again.

Errors are important precedents to build on and improve. Add place and date to each sketch and maybe a couple of words to define the context.

Something like: "Firenze, October 21, 2020. Cold and sunny."

Wherever you are going next weekend, "Bring your own sketchbook!"

06.

Let lines speak for you!

Drawing is a language, with rules, codes, but more importantly with its own grammar and orthography: in other words, it implies correctness!

Be careful: when I say correctness I am not speaking of sophisticated codes and standards. I am simply speaking of the basic conventions regulating technical drawings: thick lines, thin lines and dashed lines.

When you draw you manage an incredibly powerful tool. When you can draw something it means you can communicate it and you can learn from it. With a simple black and white drawing you can be understood everywhere in the world.

When a drawing is correct it doesn't need any captions.

You don't have to be Michelangelo to be correct; you only need clear ideas about your subject and the willingness to communicate them. The quest for correctness will teach you to expect more from your drawings. No compromises are possible when a drawing is correct. To be correct, drawings may sometime require determination and a little more time but the results for sure won't need lots of explanations to be understood. If drawings are correct, they are self-explanatory, too. As such, they will help you organize your presentation explaining why your project looks the way it looks, instead of explaining what the drawings are trying to represent.

Don't say: "This is the ground floor plan of my project ..." Instead, say: "I designed the ground floor plan of my project this way because ..."

In my most recent years working with students, I noticed that the younger generations are using the Google search engine in image mode. They rely on it, especially while abroad, as a visual dictionary.

If I don't know what a lathe is, Google will show me a picture of it; even better, it will show me a thousand pictures of lathes and I will understand that a lathe is a "*tornio*" in Italian.

Because of the language barrier, ac academic term abroad is a great opportunity to test your ability to be correct and make yourself understood by using sketches and drawings.

All architecture students should know that with a set of three linetypes one can represent anything in such a way as to be understood in the USA, in Italy as or anywhere else in the world. It's a universal language.

In front of a bifurcated section line[07], a clumsy elevation without a thick ground line or a missing dashed line in plan to show a change of level in the ceiling, a shiver always runs through my back.

[07] Section lines are the thicker lines in a drawing; they must always be closed polylines. Intersections and bifurcations are impossible.

Correctness is not formalism; it is quality.

Don't be afraid of drawing too much; be afraid of drawing without focus and goals instead. Don't take anything for granted in a drawing; misunderstanding sprouts in the unsaid.

An excellent project loses its value if burdened with graphic errors or wrong drawings.

"I drew it this way, but I meant it the other way" … Words won't help your drawing to become correct.

While abroad, architecture students deal with teachers and studio critics they have never met before. Sometimes, those teachers and critics speak naive English with a bizarre accent. They use weird words and what seem to be strange circumlocutions.

Likewise, studio critics on study abroad programs have never met their students before the beginning of any given semester and know nothing about those students' skills and abilities. Personally, I don't want to know the students' GPAs before knowing them.

This situation sometimes scares students, because they are afraid of being judged outside their usual entourages. Drawing in a correct way is a way of getting rid of this fear; when a drawing is correct it doesn't need interpretations and it doesn't leave any grey areas where misunderstandings might grow. Correctness is not affected by fashion and individual taste.

Abroad, hindered by language barriers, students have an excellent opportunity to cultivate and test the correctness of their drawings.

In 1959, apparently at the height of his career, the famous saxophonist Sonny Rollins felt pressured by his unexpected rise to fame. So, he decided to take a three year break to understand what was going on with his music and focus on perfecting his craft.

As a proud New Yorker who lived in the Lower East Side, Sonny did not have a place to practice without disturbing his neighbors. He thus resolved to isolate himself on Williamsburg Bridge with his saxophone. For about three years (every single day, in all sorts of weather) Sonny went to the bridge and spent hours there, practicing and re-learning his musical skills and cleaning his expressive patterns.

The album that sprang from those solo sessions is called *The Bridge* [08]. It didn't meet with critical acclaim. The album wasn't as groundbreaking as his audience expected.

[08] Sonny Rollins, *The Bridge*, (New York: RCA Victor, 1962).

The record tapes reveal that the withdrawal was not the bridge to a new language, as there was no renewal; rather, Sonny's withdrawal marked the arrival at a greater mastery of his own means of expression.

An academic semester abroad can be your bridge. Use that period as an opportunity to go back to basics and master them: orthographic projections, for example. In my opinion, recent architecture schools curricula are often misleading in their tendency to avoid Descriptive Geometry related arguments in favour of 3D solid modeling software. In doing so, they miss the fact that geometry is an important training field when we deal with space. Consequently, descriptive geometry can serve as an important kind of gymnastics to keep imagination and physical reality connected.

While sketching, prioritize two-dimensional drawings: plans, sections and elevations are better than perspectives if you want to understand space.

Orthogonal drawings are a better tool to understand proportions and physicality in architecture. Sketching in perspective will reduce architecture to its image, and space to its simulacrum.

It sounds like a contradiction in terms but three-dimensional drawings (like perspectives) are about two-dimensional images as two-dimensional drawings, like orthogonal projections, are about space and mass.

Not unlike a section or an elevation, a plan is an abstract drawing that can reveal the intimate nature of space. I call it "abstract" for two reasons. First, no one will ever see a section in real life. Second, it tries to extract a measurable drawing from an image (the one formed on your retinas) that is not measurable, if not by comparison. This abstraction is of incredible value in understanding space. So, whether you are inside the Pazzi Chapel or in front of your cup of coffee, force yourself to draw it in plan, section and elevation better than in perspective as it appears from your point of view.

Another interesting old school exercise is to always pair those basic drawings (plans, sections, and elevations) aligning and overturning them on the pages of your sketchbook. This way you will grasp the physical relationship and the proportional system that links them together. For instance, imagine you're trying to sketch the facade of Palazzo Rucellai. As we all know full well, it's not always possible to enter a building and verify your assumptions. So, my suggestion is: picture a small wall section next to it and a piece of plan underneath. Everything will work out smoother and faster than you can imagine.

And (trying is believing) the drawings will turn out to be more appealing and satisfying.

Also, by drawing this way, measuring with your eyes and comparing dimensions using sectional plans (whether horizontal or vertical) you will not only investigate spatial qualities but constructive constraints and materiality as well.

The next step will be adding geometrical shadows to your drawing. Notice that I'm not speaking of adding a photorealistic touch to your drawing, exactly as you do when you enable shadows in your solid modeling software. Rather, I suggest that you add a layer of information on the depth of (and between) the lines that are being used to represent your subject. So, try to add shadows, not as they are in reality but as they should look using a virtual source of distant light at a 45° angle on both horizontal and vertical directions. This way the length of the shadows will be exactly the same as the gap between the items represented in your drawing. In doing so, you'll manage to give a precise sense of depth to apparently flat elevations and plans.

Again, the interest is not so much in how things look like but in how things are. Architectural drawings are not paintings; they are not made only to be beautiful or gracious but to understand or make people (clients, contractors or builders) understand architecture. If they also happen to be beautiful, it will be an added quality.

Yet, a correct drawing of a great building is better than a beautiful drawing of a poor building.

The more a drawing will speak of architecture, space and construction, the more it will be appreciated (and leave your interlocutor speechless).

The interesting part of these suggestions is that, by refusing to represent the image of architecture you will start to represent architecture and to master the art of both managing and representing architectural space.

In other words, by forcing yourself to sketch in plan, section and elevation (using shadows and avoiding gestural attempts at creating a quick photorealistic drawing) you will learn to draw spatial subjects quickly.

It may sound strange but staying away from perspectives will make you a better perspective designer in the end.

07.

Steal! (And then return like bees do)

I don't want to encourage anyone to illegal practices or plagiarism, of course. Yet, if a thief is someone who steals another person's property (especially by stealth and without using force or threat of violence), then an architect is inevitably a thief: someone who steals ideas and knowledge from one context and takes it to another.

Under this metaphor, a semester abroad is an infinite quarry of diamonds, the perfect fuel for the engine of your imagination.

Let's face it: you can't invent the umbrella. It has been invented already. Gravity, protection from the elements, comfort, fruition, and the notion of legacy: architects have been facing these problems since the earliest times. Architects rarely invent something that is completely new. When they do, the results tend to be questionable, and—speaking of umbrellas—their roofs often

Nothing is original. Steal from anywhere that resonates with inspiration or fuels your imagination. Devour old films, new films, music, books, paintings, photographs, poems, dreams, random conversations, architecture, bridges, street signs, trees, clouds, bodies of water, light and shadows. Select only things to steal from that speak directly to your soul. If you do this, your work (and theft) will be authentic. Authenticity is invaluable; originality is non-existent. And don't bother concealing your thievery—celebrate it, if you feel like it. In any case, always remember what Jean-Luc Godard said: "It's not where you take things from—it's where you take them to."
—Jim Jarmusch

leak.[09] In architecture, extreme originality is usually interesting in the short term. However, that same speed, which boosted the infatuation for novelty, will end up triggering the obsolescence of a building. I hope you may excuse my bluntness, but I find extravagance to be a contemporary illness and the obsessive quest for originality a stupid, young demon.

In his early book on Louis Kahn (written in 1960, published a year later), Vincent Scully wrote that Kahn designing the Salk Institute Meeting House (which was eventually left incomplete) had "copied" the plan of Hadrian's Villa (which, by the way, was pinned on the wall in front of Khan's drafting table). Kahn always said he was "inspired" in that project by the plans of Hadrian's Villa, Diocletian's Palace, and other assemblies of room-buildings. Kahn was unhappy about that passage of the book. In a later interview, when asked about it, Kahn revealed that the sheer copying of forms is not in his nature: "I am not made that way", he stated. Then he went on saying that geometric forms such as the circle are available for use by all people at all times; as such, they cannot belong to any particular designer or culture.

[10] I owe this anecdote to Professor Robert McCarter, who once told me about this dispute while having dinner together in Firenze. This is a good example of the many "perks" that come from belonging to the community of educators abroad.

Eventually, Kahn finished that interview asking: **"Who owns the copyright for the circle?"**[10]

Originality and plagiarism are fake problems. As Schopenhauer put it: "The real problem is not so much to see what nobody has yet seen, as to think what nobody has yet thought concerning that which everybody sees."[11]

[11] Arthur Schopenhauer, *Parerga und Paralipomena* (Oxford: Clarendon Press, 2000) Vol. 2, Sec.761851.

Seeing the new in what already exists is called imagination. It's a skill that can (and must) be trained in architectural education—especially abroad—these days.

In an interview during a 1996 PBS documentary called "Triumph of the Nerds," Steve Jobs said: "Picasso used to say that 'Good Artists Copy, Great Artists Steal.' We have always been shameless about stealing great ideas." There is a big controversy about Picasso—or someone else—having said that. What we know for sure is that Pablo Picasso, as reported by one of his wives (Françoise Gilot, in *Life with Picasso*), used to say:" When there's anything to steal, I steal!"

I'm not going to comment any further on this controversy involving the Spanish artist and the US business magnate of industrial design. Yet I want to underline a main difference separating industrial design from art: it concerns the notions of copyright and authorship. Steve Jobs was speaking from a field ruled (and protected) by copyright laws; Pablo Picasso did not.

Luckily enough, there is no copyright in architecture, and convenience has played a crucial role in the evolution of the built environment of cities. Let's think of those theories (derived from Vitruvius' suggestion in De architectura, II.1.3) that consider the structure and decorative apparatus of the Greek temple as a transformation (in stone) of primitive buildings originally built in clay and wooden beams.

For centuries, buildings have been built copying successful solutions, only making small variations to customize use and improve performance. Huge portions of cities are built with the same basic typologies, which have been improved on by never-ending variations. Thanks to this process, some urban fabrics have reached the level of masterpieces. In Firenze, entire blocks and streets are structured by parallel bearing walls made of bricks and floors layered on top of wooden beams, pitched roofs covered in terracotta roof tiles, and plastered facades in pale colors.

The result is the city we all know.

Architecture is architecture because there is no copyright on it. We can tell the story of architecture and learn from it by peeling off its body, layer after layer. Architecture has always had a close relationship with nature and its laws: it represents both an inspiration and an enemy. As we all know, nature doesn't waste energy; it acts by convenience. Leibniz stated that *Natura non facit saltus* ("Nature does not make jumps"). Well, architecture doesn't either. Continuity makes architecture more interesting, not boring.

All architects store—so to speak—in their toolboxes masterpieces of architecture, buildings, spontaneous structures and industrial design products. A toolbox of this kind serves as an in progress set of ingenious solutions to be improved or failures to avoid.

Apprentice architects need to feed off images, concepts, and solutions. They must ask themselves about the space where they act, how it works, how it stands, what its qualities are.

In his *Scientific Autobiography* (which was written in America) Italian architect and intellectual Aldo Rossi wrote: "Perhaps the observation of things has remained my most important formal education; for observation later becomes transformed into memory. Now I seem to see all the things I have observed arranged like tools in a neat row; they are aligned as in a botanical chart, or a catalogue, or a dictionary. But this catalog, lying somewhere between imagination and memory, is not neutral; it always reappears in several objects and constitutes their deformations and, in some way, their evolution."[12]

[12] Aldo Rossi, A Scientific Autobiography, (Cambridge: MIT Press, 1982), 23.

When you are abroad (but also when at home) steal with your eyes, as often as possible.

We saw how Steve Jobs, Jim Jarmush, and Pablo Picasso all described themselves—in a sense—as thieves. In regard to architects, throughout his long career Le Corbusier often called himself a *voleur* (French for "thief"). His curiosity pushed him always to pay great attention to the things around him: nature, objects, buildings, cities and urban scenes, masterpieces as well as ordinary buildings, ancient as well as modern. If you haven't already, you should spend an afternoon in your school library flipping through the four books of Le Corbusier's *Carnets de Dessins*. They were published in 1982 by Electa (in Italy) and by The MIT Press (in the US). Bound in these four volumes are the reproductions of the 63 sketchbooks that the famous Swiss architect filled from 1914 to 1964. Those sketchbooks are the "warehouse"—so to speak—where he kept his "stolen goods" in the form of notes and sketches: impressions, bills, measures, places, details, landscapes, figures, from which his ideas and architectural designs took shape.

Since Ancient Egypt, bees have been used as symbols, bearing multiple meanings. In heraldry, for instance, the bee is a symbol of industriousness, hard work and sweetness (and hope, too, at times). The best-known "symbolic bees" are those on Napoleon's imperial cloak.

In my studio lessons I often use bees as a metaphor referring to international students. Italy is still one of the most appreciated sites for study abroad. Suffice it to say that, if we look at the number of students enrolled in US universities who went abroad in the last semester before the pandemic, more than 11% chose Italy as their destination. Also, in the 2018/2019 school year almost 40.000 university students from the US came to Italy for a semester abroad.

I like to think of these students as a huge swarm of worker bees flying up and down Italy, looking for pollen and nectar to be transformed into sweet honey once they go back to their bee-hive.

Honey is a clear expression of the context that produced it: different territories and even different seasons can return a different product with distinct peculiarities and taste somehow reflecting the conditions responsible for that specific kind of honey.

To continue my simile, architecture students abroad raid the Italian territory, stealing architectural pollen and keeping it in the wax combs that are their sketchbooks, thus transforming it into the sweet and nutritious honey of new design.

More importantly, these benefits are not limited to the production of honey. With their raids, bees also play an important role as pollinators of crops. In the realm of plants (and all the more so in agriculture) pollinators—as bees are—make production possible by transferring pollen from a male to a female part of a plant, later enabling fertilization and the production of seeds. Just to give a simple example: without bees and other pollinator insects we would not have—among other things—cherries and apples.

The one described above is a perfect case of mutualism, a circular "economy" where both actors benefit from interacting with one another. To conclude my simile, I believe that the architecture of the future must be more about creating mutualistic relationships in the built environment than about parasitizing it.

Going back to the copyright issue for a second (and to finish that topic, too): taking pictures of artworks in museums and exhibitions is often prohibited, but that does not apply (in most cases, at least) to drawing and taking notes.

So, don't be afraid: "steal" by sketching. It is still a legal practice.

And don't forget to return (in a better condition) what you stole.

Good architects should always make a positive impact on the world.

08.

Le Corbusier? Can you please spell it?

A few years ago, during a lecture in a third year studio (I won't reveal where), I cited Le Corbusier's famous five points. From the back of the classroom (at least they were listening back there) someone asked me to spell the name of the Swiss architect.

Walter Gropius made us throw away the book of architecture history. But, first, he had learned it all by heart, that bastard! –Giovanni Klaus Koenig (quote reported in one of my notes from the course in Storia dell'Architettura Contemporanea, 1989-90 academic year)

Usually the best time to go abroad in the curriculum of a School of Architecture is either the third or the fourth year. Students are by then 20 or 21 for the most part, and—in general—they are architecturally literate, although still "undercooked" as designers. This makes up a good mix, which lends itself well to such a formative experience.

Le Corbusier: "Who are you?"

When browsing Google, it seems that the round shape of the eyeglasses he used to wear is more popular than his buildings. At this point of your architectural curriculum you should be familiar with this architect's name and his contribution to the evolution of modern architecture. If not…hurry up and use the semester abroad to make up for it. Although he was not Italian, France borders on Italy and it is just a couple of hours away from Firenze by airplane. Also, about 70% of Le Corbusier remarkable buildings are within driving distance from Firenze: the best way to understand and memorize architecture is to experience it from within, as it were.

Speaking of experience and education abroad, Le Corbusier himself always considered his trip to Italy—and specifically to Firenze—a fundamental step in his architectural training.

"This experience changed my life."

In September 1907 (more precisely, Monday 15th) the twenty-year-old Charles Edouard Jeanneret Gris (aka Le Corbusier), fresh from his studies at the school of fine arts, left the Swiss town of La Chaux des Fonds and headed for Italy. The classic *"voyage en Italie"* (also known as The Grand Tour), which was typical of the nineteenth-century educational tradition, made an indelible mark in the training of this great master of modern architecture. This proved to be particularly true of his visit to the *Certosa di Ema*, a few kilometers south of Firenze. Guided by John Ruskin's Mornings in Florence (or faithfully following the suggestions of the Baedeker Guide) on a late summer day the young Le Corbusier got on a carriage of the Chianti tram headed south.

At the sight of the fourteenth-century Florentine charterhouse (located in the Galluzzo neighborhood, on the top of a cliff washed downstream by the Ema and the Greve streams) Le Corbusier had an unexpected shock!

In addition to the impressive architecture, what most struck him was the functionality of the monastic environments. Experiencing it, he was impressed by the harmonious integration between the collective spaces and the spaces for the exclusive use of the monks (namely, the cells). Analysing and studying the harmony connecting and pervading these monastic environments, the young architect made sketches and drawings to better retain them in his memory.

After visiting the Charterhouse, Le Corbusier wrote to his parents and to his teacher (Charles L'Eplattenier) reporting he had found the solution to the problem of housing for workers.

Many years later, he himself admitted that this visit would decide his whole life by making him feel more Florentine than a Florentine. In sum, it was a visit to the Carthusian monastery of Galluzzo that inspired Le Corbusier with the first idea of a new housing concept, initially modelled after the monks' cells and common areas. Eventually, that inspiration would lead to Le Corbusier's *Unitè d'Habitation* and other housing projects by him.

Not surprisingly, Le Corbusier returned to that monastery first in 1911 and then a few more times in the course of his long, brilliant career.

So, buy a bus ticket: it's only one euro and fifty cents. Jump on a 37 bus heading south and go pass a couple of hours inside the Certosa. Don't forget your sketchbook... you never know!

At the beginning of each semester, I ask the new cohort of students enrolled in my studio course what they know about Italian architecture (meaning both buildings and who designed them). The usual answer is: "Old classical stuff…"[13] Sometimes (though seldom) students may randomly name Andrea Palladio, Renzo Piano or Carlo Scarpa (the latter a great master of architecture from the fifties, despite his not being even a graduate in architecture, let alone a licensed architect).

[13] That is their "precise definition" of Italian architecture.

It goes without saying that such answers show great confusion both geographically and chronologically. And yet, Italy has always had a deep relationship with architects and architecture at least since Vitruvius (if not before that). As of today, Italy has the highest density of architects in the world. According to Rem Koolhaas's Venice Architecture Biennale *Fundamentals* (dating from 2014), there is one licensed architect every 400 inhabitants in Italy; in the US, this number goes up to more than 3000. In other words, Italy (whose surface is comparable to that of Arizona, hosting a population similar to that of California and Texas put together) has more licensed architects (150.000) than the entire USA (105.000).

Obviously, I don't want to brag about my own country. However, even just for statistical reasons, considering the huge numbers that I have just mentioned (which can prove most scary to anyone practicing architecture in this country), Italy must have had some important architects not only in the glorious distant past. There are, indeed, important and remarkable architects that I would love to suggest, both for what they built and for what they contributed to the history of architecture.

Limiting our attention to the last century, a semester in Italy is an opportunity to become familiar with such architects and places as those I will try briefly to suggest in the following pages. I'm going to list them randomly, as they spring to mind, since this is not a handbook of modern architecture in Italy. I don't pretend to offer a complete survey; for sure, I'll forget some fine architects. Yet, I have no doubts in recommending the ones I'm about to mention as cornerstones of Italian architecture in the last century.

Maybe you are among those privileged students who have already been exposed to the work of **Carlo Scarpa** through architecture books. Even in this case, though, a weekend (or, why not, a Spring Break) in the Veneto is an easy suggestion. Here are some destinations and the related works to visit: **Verona** for Castelvecchio and the Banco Popolare, **Altivole** with the Brion Cemetery and **Possagno** with the Gipsoteca Canoviana, maybe ending in **Venezia** for the Fondazione Querini Stampalia, the entrance to the Tolentini building (IUAV headquarters) and the Olivetti shop in Piazza San Marco.

Como should be another destination for an architectural weekend. There one can visit almost all the buildings designed and built by **Giuseppe Terragni**, one of the fathers of Italian modern architecture. If you don't have a full weekend, make sure to save at least a couple of hours for a coffee break in front of the Casa del Fascio. If this architect's name doesn't sound familiar and I haven't convinced you yet, please ask for credits to Peter Eisenmann at Yale or read (since the author, unfortunately, is no longer with us) Thomas Schumaker's seminal book on Terragni[14].

Their English is way better than mine and their arguments are certainly more convincing.

[14] T.L. Schumacher, *Surface and Symbol. Giuseppe Terragni and the Architecture of Italian Rationalism* (New York: Princeton Architectural Press, 1991).

Like Como, **Milano** is a perfect candidate for an architecture/design weekend, both because of its glamorous fashion boutiques and for being one of the cradles of Italy's so-called "mild modernity." This formula alludes to a kind of modernity that—though challenged by both technical and linguistic innovations—manages to be respectful of local traditions and of the city's urban fabric. **Ernesto Nathan Rogers** was the director of Casabella during the reconstruction in the aftermath of World War II, when this journal was significantly retitled Casabella Continuità. With friends and colleagues **Banfi, Belgioioso** and **Peressutti,** in 1932 he founded **BBPR** (the first firm, to the best of my knowledge, whose name is an acronym made of the initials of the partners involved, predating SOM by a couple of years and well before HOK, OMA, MVRDV and all the other design groups that have been so trendy lately). I urge you to visit their Torre Velasca and see how they set up the museum inside the Castello Sforzesco.

If you have time, I suggest that book a visit to the "casa-studio Castiglioni" (right outside the Castello Sforzesco). This design office has stood out as a creative crucible for more than 50 years now. There one can still feel the presence of **Pier Giacomo** and **Achille Castiglioni**. These two brothers are a brilliant example of what the word "design" means in Italy.

Walking around in Milano, please give yourselves the opportunity to take a look at some buildings by **Luigi Caccia Dominioni**, an architect I'm not afraid to consider among the most copied in recent years. Caccia Dominioni has been a gifted and consistently productive architect who contributed to shaping the new housing typology in Milano during the 1960s economic boom. He was more interested in having a professional dialogue with his clients and contractors than with scholars and critics. Maybe this is the reason why his name (both in Italy and abroad) was very little known until recently. His ability at combining the lightness of modernity and the solidity of tradition with a sober elegance has recently become of great interest among architects and scholars. This has led to a sort of underground cult in the contemporary design scene that sees Caccia Dominioni's contribution as a potential way out of architecture's stagnation today. On the way back to the Stazione Centrale, before jumping on the train, take a picture (or, even better, make a sketch) of the Grattacielo Pirelli, which stands right opposite the train station's main facade. Together with the Torre Velasca, this tall building (designed by the prolific architect **Gio Ponti** in 1956) is among the first examples of "modern towers" built in Italy. Italians regard it as a skyscraper (*"grattacielo"*) but if you have been to Manhattan it will look like a toy to you. At any rate, it still stands out in the skyline of Milano as a manifesto of elegance and majesty, way more than many contemporary skyscrapers do.

Another protagonist of the Milanese scene and of the cultural debate on post-war reconstruction in Italy is **Ignazio Gardella**. Many of his buildings became icons of a different modernity that ran counter to the then dominant European trends influenced by so-called International Style. Buildings like the Casa alle Zattere in **Venezia**, the Borsalino housing complex and the Anti-Tuberculosis Hospital in **Alessandria** or the School of Architecture in **Genova** are seminal examples of an Italian way to modern architecture. As such, they are all worth a small detour.

Genova is another potential weekend trip. The area around the Porto Vecchio (the Old Seaport, which **Renzo Piano** started to redesign in 1992) is very interesting, as it shows examples of functional and linguistic integration between old and new. While in Genova, underneath the cathedral of San Lorenzo you can find a real masterpiece. I'm speaking of the museum dedicated to the treasure (mostly precious reliquaries) owned by this church. Designed in 1952 by **Franco Albini** (another architect from the Milanese scene of the 1950s), this structure itself is worth the cost of a visit to Genova. If you feel that this is not enough yet, then you can visit the museums of Palazzo Bianco and Palazzo Rosso, both installed inside two palazzos on the Strada Nuova (an important example of Renaissance urban design by Galeazzo Alessi).

During your stay in **Firenze**, in addition to the many local masterpieces dating from the Middle Ages and the Renaissance, you can find important buildings designed by **Giovanni Michelucci**. Michelucci has been a true "maestro" for several generations of Florentine architects. I suggest that you take a moment (maybe before or after a train trip) to appreciate his Santa Maria Novella railway station. I also urge you to pay a visit to the building that he designed at the corner between Via Guicciardini and Via dello Sprone, to his project for the Cassa di Risparmio (a bank) on Via Bufalini and the Post Office building on via Pietrapiana. Last but not least, spend a morning visiting the Church of San Giovanni Battista, also known as the "highway church" in **Campi Bisenzio**. Being located a few kilometers outside Florence, it's not easy to reach; yet, this innovative project is a must-see for any architect.

It is difficult to visit **Mario Ridolfi's** buildings unless you don't go to **Terni**, a small town between Umbria and Lazio. But if you google "Mario Ridolfi

Drawings", you will be surprised (in fact, I believe, astonished) by the results. You'll find hundreds of beautiful drawings, carefully handcrafted not to be beautiful or to be framed and pinned on the wall but to be helpful instead. For instance, helpful for architects to clarify and evolve their ideas, helpful for builders to understand how and what to do, helpful for anyone else to understand architecture. Finally, Ridolfi's drawings are helpful for us to have an alternative to the contemporary standardized and boring realm of digital renderings.

From Firenze in a couple of hours by train you can easily reach **Perugia**, a little medieval town in Umbria. Once there, don't miss a visit to Piazza IV Novembre. If you like sweets and happen to be in Italy for the Fall Semester, I recommend that you visit Perugia during the Eurochocolate week. Eurochocolate is an "epic" chocolate festival that takes place outdoors in Perugia's historic district. Still on this topic, Perugia is best known for the Perugina chocolate factory, which gave birth—in 1922—to the famous *Bacio* ("kiss" in English). A romantic hazelnut chocolate, each Bacio is wrapped up in a love-note. On your way from the Perugia train station to the city center, you'll pass through Piazza del Bacio. This complex was designed in 1983 by **Aldo Rossi,** the first Italian architect to win the Pritzker Prize. Seeking dialogue and integration with the past, this Milanese architect designed a long brick-paved pedestrian square that follows the natural slope of the terrain, which is typical of many piazzas in Italian historic cities (for instance, **Siena** and **Arezzo**, both worth a visit, just to name two of them) with a fountain in the center. Among the buildings in this piazza, as a memory, Rossi left standing one of the old chimneys of the original Perugina factory.

As a side note, to reach the historic district of Perugia I suggest that you take the mini metro (designed by Jean Nouvel) and the escalators inside the ancient fortress called Rocca Paolina (an interesting example of modern urban infrastructural intervention within an historical context).

Urbino is the hometown of Raphael and the urban masterpiece of Francesco di Giorgio Martini. The latter's Palazzo Ducale hosts one of the most important national museums of Italy; there you can admire— among other famous paintings and artworks—Piero della Francesca's *Flagellazione di Cristo* (The Flogging of Christ) and one of the notorious views (together with those in Baltimore's Walters Art Museum and in Berlin's Gemäldegalerie) of the *Citta Ideale*. This may not sound enough to justify a long weekend in Urbino. However, an architecture student should certainly add to the "to see list" for the weekend in this small town the buildings that **Giancarlo De Carlo** designed for the local university in the historic district. Il Magistero and the Facoltà di Legge are real gems in showing how transform historical buildings to serve new, contemporary purposes. Moreover, as a student you can rent for a very low fee a room in the Il Colle dorm, one of the four dorms on the Urbino University campus. In my opinion, the best dorm is the one designed and built by De Carlo on the hill opposite the historic district.

Usually, **Capri** and the Costiera Amalfitana are among the top five destinations that American students look forward to visiting when they come to Italy. If you go to Capri, I suggest that you book your ferry from Salerno; this way you can visit (and use) the new maritime station designed by Zaha Hadid. As an architecture student, while on the island of Capri don't miss the opportunity to take a look at **Adalberto Libera**'s Casa Malaparte. This house was designed for the Italian writer Curzio Malaparte on the cliff of Capo Massullo. Although one can only see it from the outside, Casa Malaparte is a treasure worth the detour from the usual stereotyped tour of the island.

As an architecture student, if you are spending your semester abroad in Italy, you must go to the capital (at least twice). Between the majestic ancient ruins and Michelangelo's masterpieces, while in **Roma** try to save some time and go to the Eur to visit Libera's Palazzo dei Congressi, dating from 1953.

At the Eur, I suggest you go see an Italian basketball match; it won't be anything like the NBA, of course, but the Palazzetto dello Sport (aka Palaeur) and its concrete structure stands out as an absolute masterpiece by **Pier Luigi Nerv**i, who was both a great Italian architect and an engineer. If you prefer soccer (*calcio* in Italian) to basketball and you happen to go see a Fiorentina match at the Stadio Comunale Artemio Franchi in Firenze, please take some time to observe and sketch the spiral staircases of the Maratona bleachers: they are a stroke of genius by this designer. Unfortunately, most tourist guides fail to mention that. Going back to the title of this chapter, Le Corbusier once said: "Seeing Nervi placing a concrete structure in a building is a magnificent lesson. He never puts anything vulgar into it. What elegance! He doesn't call himself an architect, but he's better than most of us."

These (named randomly, without pretending to be complete) are just a few places, buildings and architects that I feel obliged to include in the "to do lists" for my students, so that they can bring them back home after a semester of architecture school in Italy.

If asked again about architecture in Italy, their answers will be more focused and articulated.

And they will be aware that the italian contribution to Architecture did not end with Bernini and Borromini.

At least, I hope so.

09.

Fall in love!

This suggestion might sound lovey dovey and stereotyped. It may recall romantic movies like *Under the Tuscan Sun* or *A Room with a View*.[15]

Some students (actually, a remarkable percentage, according to a recent research by Expatica.com) see the semester abroad as an adventurous opportunity to flirt with good-looking foreigners or have exciting, romantic temporary "affairs" in foreign cities. Obviously, the next pages won't discuss this kind of activities. I am an architecture professor, not some kind of "love therapist." Unfortunately, I don't have that kind of background.

Love happens when it happens, at home or abroad. Wait to make plans about love until it happens. Coming to Firenze with the hidden intent of finding a new Italian boyfriend or girlfriend can never be a winning path.

You're abroad; so, be abroad. You're in Firenze; so, be in Firenze.

The kind of love I'm suggesting here is simply the love of/for Architecture. Why don't you take the semester abroad as an opportunity to date

[15] Under the Tuscan Sun (113 min.) by Audrey Wells, 2004 and A Room with a View (115 min) by James Ivory, 1985. The former is definitely shallow while the latter is more convincing. In any case, they are both to be seen, before or after a semester abroad in Firenze.

Love architecture, both old and modern. Love it for its fantastic, adventurous, and solemn creations; for its inventions; for the abstract, allusive, and figurative forms that enchant our spirit and enrapture our thoughts. Love architecture, the stage and the support of our life.

–Gio Ponti, *In praise of Architecture*

Architecture? If you want this kind of love, stop going to the bar where every other student abroad goes. Take a walk outside, go to a library, visit every museum, get lost. Fill your days with new and exciting urban adventures and lots of sketches.

Architecture is your field of studies; don't treat it as a boring duty. It should be your life from now on.

We are living in a world made of sanitized stereotyped performances and aseptic impersonal relationships, where showing passion and excitement for a subject is often seen as synonymous with weakness. In architecture school, passion for studying this subject is often seen by peers as a nerd attitude. But architecture school is not high school; here you do things mainly for yourself (or, at least, for your portfolio). Before bringing your design to a desk crit and see if you are moving in the right direction, ask yourself if you feel in the right direction.

Are you really proud of your product?

Don't be ashamed to show your passion, your enthusiasm in approaching design. There is a huge need for these feelings; a School of Architecture should be a training field for them.

Quoting Adolf Loos, we can say that Architecture is able to arouse sentiments in humans. If Architecture is not able to trigger sentiments in you, how can you make your own Architecture arouse sentiments in others?

Honestly, I'm confident that passion and sympathy for Architecture are among the professional skills that will soon be highly appreciated in professional profiles.

Unlike many colleagues of mine, I don't see architecture as the center of the world and architects as semi-gods. I simply think that space, the quality of space, is currently underrated because of mainstream virtuality. Nevertheless, we have a biological need for space. Our lives happen in space and the quality of space can improve our lives in this world.

Economists say: "Buy low, sell high." So, if I should tell a young architect what—in my opinion— is going to pay off in today's architectural education, I'd say: Love, Passion, and Storytelling. Their value is underestimated at the moment but it will start going up sooner than you can imagine. Signs of these trends are already visible.

People have lost interest in Architecture, but they love to see things through the Architect's eyes and hear stories created by our imagination. Today, people need to be re-educated in space and architecture through passionate (and nicely told) stories.

Use the time you spend in Architecture school to improve these skills: if you are not able to share your feelings with your teachers and peers during design studios, how will you be able to share them with your clients in the near future? Photorealistic renderings and virtual reality are becoming standardized and cheap; as a result, their quotations in portfolios are already going down. From the feedback I got from students in some twenty years of teaching, I realized that study abroad projects provide excellent conversational material for interviews, way more than renderings.

Using Roman Jakobson's six functions of language, tomorrow's portfolios will need the Emotive function more than the Referential one. They will speak and add information about the speaker's passion without altering the denotative meaning of the drawings and the projects chosen to represent the author.

Interviews will be **more focused on who you are than what you can do**.

Why is a semester abroad (especially in Italy) a great opportunity to practice the Emotive function?

The answer is: Because Italy is still a truly romantic place.

It is certainly true that—generally speaking—Italian people are passionate, romantic and culturally very outgoing. Like all languages stemming from Latin, Italian is commonly referred to as a "*Romance language*." Often paired with love and passion, the words Romantic and Romance (with all their attached meanings) come from the word Rome. In the Middle Ages, French poets wrote in *Romanz* (their old Latin derivative vernacular) about chivalrous and gallant knights.

Passionate, colorful and articulate, the Italian language is often not enough to fully express topics; exuberant hand gestures and expressive body language are a common part of every conversation in the *Belpaese*. And this passion is not limited to interpersonal relationships. Everything in Italy is the result of a unique combination of gusto, joie de vivre, energy, and—of course—passion!

If something of this passion is still alive in Italy, then there is no better place to practice the emotive function.

10.

Style is a way to say who you are.

Find your voice!

There is capital "S" Style and lower case "s" style.

Style is a word that shouldn't have a plural.

We often swap style with language, but Style has more to do with spirit and authenticity than with language. Capital "S" Style involves humans in all their aspects, not only notional or professional ones; it is the result of their experiences and their culture.

As Yves Saint Lauren used to say: "*Fashions—like architecture styles—fade; Style is eternal.*"

Your designs and your drawings are speaking of you as much as your sneakers or your haircut do. Be as ashamed of presenting a drawing you are not proud of as you would be if you wore an ugly sweater far from Christmas season..

Capital "S" Style is an attitude (the result of a long process of sedimentation and selection, both vivid and always evolving); style, instead, is a form (static and immutable).

Abroad you can study the history of architecture in person without pictures or videos. You can have a physical experience of the space hidden inside the pictures of the masterpieces that you are used to admiring in books or on-line. This way it is easier to understand the difference between Architecture and its image. Between Style and style.

Pay respect to the "masters," learn how to use history as a design tool, as an inspiration and not as a language to be copied passively.

Be humble; you are a student.

Listen to your teachers and design tutors; try to follow their instructions even if they seem odd or unusual. Only after following these suggestions, argue—if you wish—and stand on your own two feet.

Make an effort to understand local traditions. If you do so, you shall realize that what looks "normal" is not so "normal." Traditions are the result of an infinite series of improvements, tested over a long period of time. As Adolf Loos stated: "Even if it is hundreds of years old, truth has a stronger inner bond with us than the lie that walks by our side."

The goal of studying abroad is not to become fluent in a design language different than the one you are used to. The goal of studying abroad is to be exposed to diversity and to start a negotiation with it.

My goal while teaching Architecture Design Studio is not to teach a style or to share my language. I don't have such a "strong" language to feel compelled to articulate it. Besides, I think that reducing architectural design to the definition of a universal language is obsolete and uninteresting.

When abroad we have the opportunity to acquire awareness of the changes that are going on in the present, both inside and outside Architecture. Art, books, cinema, sports, lifestyle, science, fashion, food, love, politics, everything (if considered in an authentic and sincere vein) can contribute to your voice. Organizing and composing diversities is more prolific than merging them into a unique picture.

Speaking of Style, as a reflection, I suggest investing one day of your semester in Florence to pay a visit to the Stefano Bardini Museum and its artworks.

To find them you must head toward the Oltrarno part of town, passing through Ponte alle Grazie. From the bridge, looking south and up, you can see a portion of the facade of Palazzo Bardini. Further up, past Palazzo Mozzi, are the Bardini Gardens, crowned by the Loggia Belvedere and the Villa Bardini. Further away, standing out against the skyline, one can see the medieval silhouette of the Torre del Gallo, which is also part of the Bardini property.

Thanks to his knowledge of art history, his ability in talking about it, and—most importantly—capitalizing on the opportunity offered by living in Florence during the big renovations that impacted its historic district in the years between the XIX and XX centuries, Stefano Bardini accumulated an invaluable patrimony consisting in both artworks and real estate.

This Florentine antiquarian purchased and started renovating the Villa, the Garden, and the Palace (today all open to visitors as museums) in the 1880s. His goal was to transform this part of Florence into a real "showroom" of antiquities, a sort of full-scale showcase to display and stage his impressive collection for potential buyers.

In addition to being an antiquarian, a collector, and an art dealer, Stefano Bardini was a painter and a restorer. His importance as a figure in the Florentine art world in the late XIX century can hardly be exaggerated. Although somewhat controversial, he certainly played a crucial role in defining a new and "modern" international identity for Firenze.

In the years between 1860 and the end of the century, with the great transformations planned by Poggi to morph the city into the modern capital of Italy, it was easy to find vestiges belonging to the various historical ages of Firenze among the buildings destined for demolition and to buy them for a few *Lire* ("pennies"). Medieval *fondo oro*, Roman marble decorations, portals and mantelpieces in *pietra serena* as well as *strappati* frescoes dating from the Renaissance suddenly became accessible and available for buyers on the art market. In this context, Stefano Bardini first built himself a reputation and then a fortune, becoming a world-famous leading figure in that line of business within a few years.

Bardini collected art pieces from every age and style to offer them to his international wealthy clients. When the market required it, he did not hesitate to commission works "in style" or tricky restorations, where boundaries between restoring, inventing and producing fake were blurred.

Many *strappi* of historical frescoes to be restored (as well as *strappi* of commissioned and artfully aged frescoes) are due to Bardini.

It's also revealing of Bardini's personality that he showcased the collected art pieces (ranging from sculpture to pediments, from paintings to everyday objects, from wooden ceilings to pieces of furniture) without taking into account any chronological or philological criteria. He simply followed his own taste with the sole purpose of making that unique collection attractive and appealing to potential buyers.

In doing so, he invented a new way of exhibiting art and antiquities. He realized that the works were not always purchased for the importance of the piece in itself, but also for the context in which they were placed and for the atmosphere they were able to recreate.

With inspired ease, he often decided to skilfully mix and match different objects to create a sort of "scene." In the same spirit (sometimes resorting to questionable means), he used to combine works that were different in age and origin so as to create completely new, finished pieces.

In other words, using heterogeneous authentic historic finds and combining them according to his own personal taste in a surreal and anti-historic fashion, he invented a style often known as "Florentine abroad." In fact, it was his own, personal Style: the Bardini Style. Eventually the Bardini Style (an arbitrary pastiche of Florentine artistic experiences) influenced the taste of an entire era to a greater extent than is usually recognized.

An emblematic component of the Bardini Style was the so-called "Bardini Blue." Even more emblematic and intriguing is the story of this color, which became something like the hallmark of this Florentine antique dealer. He painted (although it would be more appropriate to say "he frescoed" or "he plastered", because this was the technique used to give depth and vibrancy to the color) most of the interior walls of his building with various shades of an intense blue, tending to cornflower.

This chromatic choice was certainly dictated by functional and scenographic reasons: it was a perfect background for both the whiteness of the ancient marbles and for the gold leaf covered medieval frames and backgrounds (both of which abounded in Bardini's collection). Also, Bardini was right in thinking that his wealthy Russian customers would appreciate it, knowing that they usually chose that color for their interiors.

From the interiors of St. Petersburg to those of Palazzo Bardini, the fascination for this color made its way to the most famous collectors' residences of the time, which eventually became museums. For instance, we find it in Paris (in the rooms dedicated to Renaissance art at the Musée Jacquemart-André) and in Boston (in the rooms of the Isabella Stewart Gardner Museum). It is no coincidence that Nélie Jacquemart and Isabella Stewart Gardner were both frequenters of Palazzo Bardini and clients of Stefano Bardini. In some remarkable letters Miss Isabella repeatedly and insistently asked her Florentine consultant (the famous art historian Bernard Berenson, who lived at Villa I Tatti in Settignano) for samples and explanations about the composition of that particular color. In one such letter she writes: "And will you please some day, get on a piece of paper the blue color that Bardini has on his walls? I want that exact tint."[16]

[16] Letter to George Berenson , March 4th, 1900 in Rollin van N. Hadley, *The Letters of Bernard Berenson and Isabella Stewart Gardner* (Boston: Northeastern University Press, 1987) 207.

Bardini Blue and Bardini Style. These contributions from Stefano Bardini gave life to an innovative and recognizable identity. Far from being an eclectic language (as it has often been superficially defined), it was an original Style, a taste produced by experience, convenience, and opportunity, capable of metabolizing the stratified historical and artistic environment of Firenze while giving it a new, cosmopolitan, and vibrant life.

In sum, a Style made of many experiences and styles where local and global, present and past are intertwined.

11.

Flip it over!

Living outside our comfort zone can result in a good test to try an entirely different lifestyle.

A semester abroad in Italy is not a trip to Italy; it means living in Italy for a whole academic semester. It's not a mere list of to see and do lists that must be flagged out as fast as possible in order to accomplish more. A semester abroad offers the opportunity to look at things from a different perspective.

While abroad you can broaden your sight and break your conventions.

Be careful! This is neither a criticism of your habits nor an apology of Italian lifestyle. This is just an exhortation to discover diversity, to discover that people can do the same things in many different ways with the same conviction. Sometimes the exoticism of some habits will raise hilarity and will strengthen your position, sometimes it will be weakened by them. In the process, you will surely become aware of diversity and relativity. Abroad you will nurture respect for otherness, which is one of the major challenges to survive in a globalized world (especially as a designer).

The first time I flew to the United States was back in 2006. On the plane from Munich to New York City I realized I was flying over Ireland. This didn't make any sense according to the idea of geography that I had learned from school books, where meridians and parallels are always straight lines and interest is focused on the land. But when I ideally placed my point of view above the spherical surface of the globe between take off and landing, then I realized that the shorter route is passing over Ireland.

As a matter of fact, if you stretch a rubber band between Munich and New York City it will pass across Ireland. For convenience's sake, your airplane will take off heading north even if New York City's longitude is west and its latitude is lower than Munich's. In the end, it's a matter of points of view.

Try never to look at something in the same way twice. If you're sure about doing something in a certain way, maybe it's just because you always did it that way.

Flip it over! Force yourself to think about it in another way, to look at it from behind, even if you tend to think it's wrong or silly. When you are abroad, this process is easier because everything looks unusual.

Try alternatives and risk walking new grounds. Don't try to make your semester abroad as close as possible to your expectations. In design it's important to always go beyond appearance and conventions, testing your original idea in different scenarios.

The main challenge with design is the possibility to open our potential to confront a complex reality.

Contradictions are allowed when dealing with complexity. Design is about navigating complex scenarios, considering as many alternatives as possible and then choosing the only solution that construction requires. Sometimes successfully, sometimes unsuccessfully. Nothing is granted but chances for success become higher when we broaden our view and consider a bigger picture, where more options are possible.

Art and science have the wonderful ability of unveiling and revealing things that are usually hidden. For centuries Firenze has been a venue for art and science; it's one of the cities that have paved—so to speak—the road for western culture. Near the Uffizi Gallery and Palazzo Vecchio art collections, along the Arno river, there is one of the most important science museums in Italy: the Galileo Museum. It may not be in the top ten list for the many "two-day tourists" who flock to Firenze. Yet, it's certainly an important stop for a student who is here for a semester. Galileo Galilei has been one of the fathers of both modern science and the modern way of looking at things. For those of you who don't remember the main facts in his life, in 1633 the Inquisition of the Roman Catholic Church forced Galileo to recant his theory that the Earth moves around the Sun. The famous biblical passage "Sun, stand thou still upon Gibeon; and thou, Moon, in the valley of Aijalon"[17] as well as other passages in Scripture supported the so-called "Geocentric model," In sum, what

---

[17] Joshua 10, 12-14.

Galileo was trying to do was flip over age-old beliefs. In the end, under threat of torture, he recanted in front of his inquisitors.

When you walk into the Galileo Museum, past the entrance (recently redesigned by architects Guicciardini and Magni), I suggest that your first stop be on the second floor. There, after climbing two ramps of staircases, you'll be greeted by Sir Galileo's mummified middle finger encased in a glass vase. I like to imagine Galileo's bearded face smiling friendly, without resentment, yet indulging in foul language and gross humor for a second: *Fuck you guys! I told you: it's the Earth that moves around the Sun, not the opposite.*

Only stupid people never change their minds.

Galileo served in Firenze the lifelong house arrest that the inquisition imposed on him after his famous recantation. On a sunny Sunday morning you can take a walk to Arcetri. Climbing up Costa San Giorgio from Santa Felicita, you will visit some beautiful hidden corners and some unusual sights of the city. First, you'll pass in front of a house that Galileo bought in 1634. Bearing an oval portrait of him on the facade, it's commonly known as the *Casa di Galileo*, although he never lived there. Then you'll reach Villa Il Gioiello, where Galileo spent the last years of his life, from 1631 to his death in 1642.

Close to the garden of Villa Il Gioiello is the Arcetri Observatory, an astrophysical observatory built in 1872 and still involved in research activities, mainly relating to the study of the Sun, the stars and—in general—astrophysics. The observatory was built on this hill in the outskirts of Firenze so that observations would not be disturbed by the light and dust of the city.

This Sunday morning will be an opportunity to realize how close—even today—the quiet Tuscan country is to the center of Firenze. Also, it will help you "purify yourself" in an environment that is not haunted by tourists.

12.

Fly high! Or at least raise your sights.

Leon Battista Alberti was an early Renaissance intellectual. He had a deep impact on the Florentine scene of that time. One could say he was among the first "modern" architects of the western world.

A man of culture, a thinker and a theorist, in 1452 Alberti finished his treatise on architecture. As the title suggests (*De re aedificatoria*), Alberti wrote it in Latin. At the time, Latin was an elitarian language that only a few people (mostly Church dignitaries, highly educated aristocrats, and scholars) could master. However, by the 1450s the Italian vernacular (also known as *volgare*, i.e. the "vulgar language") could boast an already remarkable tradition, having been used for nearly two centuries to author books (and masterpieces) of various kinds and on many different subjects. In the early 1430s, Alberti himself chose the Italian vernacular to write a short, highly innovative treatise on painting (which, significantly enough, he soon translated into Latin).

As for Alberti's built projects, they were commissioned by the most important families of his time. Alberti's way of being an architect was particularly linked to conception and design. On construction sites, he always chose to have by his side fellow architects who would assist him to translate his own projects into stone.

Here are a few of those collaborators and patrons: Bernardo Rossellino in Firenze with the Rucellai and in Pienza with Pope Pius II Piccolomini, Luca Fancelli in Mantova with the Gonzagas, Matteo de' Pasti in Rimini with the Malatestas.

Around 1450, Matteo de' Pasti (one of the last specimens of the "artist-architect" figure) made a bronze medal bearing Alberti's profile.[18]

As a model, Pasti used a self-portrait Alberti made. Pasti's medal shows Alberti on one side and his iconic logo on the other. The two sides together can be said to sum up the artist's personality, his attitude to architecture and culture in general.

[18] The medallion of Leon Battista Alberti by Matteo de' Pasti (1404–72), 1446/50, Bronze, diameter 9.3 cm (3 11/16 in.) is now at the National Gallery of Art, Washington, DC, Samuel H. Kress Collection.

The logo is a Winged Eye, the eye of the architect who can see from afar, in time and space, hovering above matter, freed from gravity.

For an architect, to design means finding ways to hide thoughts inside forms, to generate shapes that express meaning.

For this reason, architects should train at once their brains (in order to think) and their hands (in order to manipulate forms).

The former is a speculative exercise dealing with theory, immateriality, and lightness; the latter is a physical exercise dealing with visibility, materiality, and gravity.

One exercise raises you to the realm of ideas, the other brings you down to earth.

Both are necessary to nurture your imagination.

An imagination only fed by memes from social media and suggestions from tour operator catalogues can hardly conceive intriguing projects.

Use your semester abroad to look up a little higher than usual and become more demanding with yourself.

In British slang a Pub Crawl is a tour where a group of people try to visit as many pubs as possible in one night, having a set number of alcoholic beverages in each. Like other famous study abroad destinations, Firenze—"Florence", as tour operators call it—is full of "young and experienced companies dedicated to creating unforgettable experiences for students abroad through tours, excursions and other activities."[19]

They offer everything needed to make time abroad unforgettable. In this context, the classic, infamous pub crawl plays an important role: apparently, it's one of the things you must do in a new city.

19 From https://www. smarttrip.it/en, the website of one of the tour operators working with students abroad.

The result is: nights spent abusing cheap alcohol in a competitive mood, headaches, and missing the opportunity to realize what's going on around.

In Firenze there are up to seventy four museums and a lot of cultural institutions: theaters, concert halls, movie theaters, exhibition areas, and libraries. All these can keep you busy and contribute to developing your sensitivity.

Firenze can also provide enough entertainment for your senses without the need for guided tours (or distorting your perception of reality). The city offers other interesting routines and paths to be walked aimlessly, enjoying every single bit of it and (why not?) tasting a couple of good drinks.

It goes without saying that this is a far cry from the Baudelairesque *flaneur*, whose goal was to wander around with no other purpose than acting as an acute observer of society. Likewise, what I'm speaking of has nothing to do with the *derive*, the technique of drifting through varied urban ambiances theorized by Guy Dabord and the Situationist International in the late 1950s.

The closest Italian idiom to translate the "crawl" would the *il giro delle sette chiese* (literally, "the tour of the seven churches"), that is, to waste a lot of time by going hither and thither.

"The tour of the seven churches" is a religious tradition dating back to 1540, when San Filippo Neri started it as a sign of Christian devotion. It consisted in the pilgrimage to the seven oldest and most important basilicas of Rome: S. Giovanni in Laterano, S. Maria Maggiore, S. Pietro in Vaticano, S. Paolo Fuori le Mura, S. Croce in Gerusalemme, S. Lorenzo Fuori le Mura, and S. Sebastiano. The distance between these seven basilicas (about 20 km, half a marathon) was expected to be covered in just one day, that is, Holy Thursday, In fact, it took two days to "go see all seven churches."

Mixing holy and profane, high and low, entertainment and education, relaxation and competitive walk, what about a Firenze Piazza Crawl?

A *Giro delle 14 Piazze*, where in a couple of hours (or along the 14 weeks of the semester, so you have more time to sketch) you can walk and sit down in 14 different Florentine piazzas. Starting in Piazza Santa Maria Novella, stopping in the Albertian triangular piazza between the Palazzo and the Loggia Rucellai, discovering the small Piazza del Limbo and then heading for Piazza del Carmine, Piazza Santo Spirito, Piazza Pitti,

Piazzetta Santa Felicita, the small piazza in the middle of Ponte Vecchio, Piazza Signoria, Piazza Santa Croce, Piazza San Firenze, Piazza Duomo, and Piazza San Lorenzo.

Maybe ending it with a Negroni (only one and only if you are 18 years old, since this is the legal drinking age in Italy) in one of the old bars in Piazza della Repubblica.

Unfortunately, the bar where it was invented doesn't exist anymore.[20]

Legend has it that Count Cammillo Negroni (an eclectic and fancy Florentine aristocrat from the early twentieth century) asked bartender Fosco Scarselli—who ran the then famous Caffé Casoni, selling also groceries and perfumes— to strengthen his Americano cocktail. The later was a very popular drink at the time; it was prepared by mixing vermouth, bitters, and soda. To pep up his "Americano cocktail", Negroni suggested the bartender that he replace soda with gin. This (he said) would give it more alcohol without altering its brilliant purple color.

To have a drink (not necessarily an alcoholic one) can be an elegant social

[20] The Caffè Casoni was founded in 1815 at the corner between Via de' Tornabuoni and Via della Spada. It was bought and transformed into the Bar Giacosa in the first decades of the twentieth century. In 2001 the Bar Giacosa was incorporated (as a small elegant bar) inside the Enrico Cavalli flagship store. In 2017, this bar closed down. It was soon turned into what is now a Giorgio Armani boutique.

gesture, much better than a bragging competitive gesture.

This is also something you can learn during your time abroad.

13.

Get your hands dirty!

In the previous chapter I spoke of the need for an architect to be an intellectual and to feed his/her imagination on theory and abstraction. In the Flip it over! chapter, instead, I wrote that contradictions are inevitable when dealing with complexity. In the same vein, I'm now going to suggest

Architecti est scientia pluribus disciplinis et variis eruditionibus ornata, cuius iudicio probantur omnia quae ab ceteris artibus perficiuntur opera.[21]

–Vitruvius, *De Architectura*

a somewhat provocative contradiction. That is, my intention in this new chapter is to describe the architect as a maker rooted in materiality and visibility (in all the senses of these words, including the most popular and physical ones).

Filippo Brunelleschi was an ingenious maker of the early Renaissance, maybe one of the last "master builders" of the Middle Ages, although he no longer practiced a merely "mechanical" art, but a "liberal art" instead (namely, one based on the knowledge of mathematics, geometry, and history).

[21] "The architect's expertise is enhanced by many disciplines and various sorts of specialized knowledge—all the works executed using these other skills are evaluated by his seasoned judgment." –Vitruvius, *Ten Books on Architecture*, translated by Ingrid D. Rowland (Cambridge: Cambridge University Press, 1999), 21.

We cannot rely on a rich corpus of drawings or models illustrating all of Brunelleschi's works. He did not write theoretical treatises in Latin, even if he is duly regarded as one of the fathers of perspective. He always preferred to express himself through his material works, whether they be buildings or machines.

As reported by Antonio Manetti (his first biographer), Filippo Brunelleschi was always on the construction sites of his projects. He used instant models made of mud, wax, wood or even carved into turnips that he would later cook. Nobody knows if this was a way to protect his innovative ideas (still shrouded in mystery) or if it was meant to help Brunelleschi communicate more effectively with his workers, who—unlike Leon Batista Alberti's clients—didn't know a word of Latin.

I like to picture Brunelleschi's hands as the calloused, dirty and strong hands of a worker, and not as those (slim and perfectly clean) of a philosopher. His genius showed in all the fields he covered, from architecture to sculpture, goldsmithery and the making of scaffoldings. He installed ovens in the construction site of the *cupolone* (the dome of Florence Cathedral). In them, bricks were backed and—shortly before lunch time—also the *Peposo all'Imprunetina*.[22] This way workers would eat their meal on the spot, without wasting time.

Hybridizing knowledge is the key for success today as it was thousands of years ago.

High and low must be kept close; mixing them can boost for view of things in unpredictable ways. If you are particularly demanding with

[22] Peposo all'Imprunetina is a kind of meat stew originally from Impruneta. A small town 10 km south of Firenze, Impruneta is mostly famous for the production of terracotta tiles and bricks. The labourers at Impruneta's furnaces used to slow cook chunks of secondary meat cuts in terracotta pots with red wine and lots

of pepper corns. The latter were meant to cover the unappealing smell of cheap meat. Once cooked this way for a long time, those meat cuts eventually become tender and saucy. On Brunelleschi's construction site for the dome of Florence Cathedral, the same ovens were used both to bake bricks and cook peposo all'Imprunetina. If you are not a vegetarian or a vegan, I recommend that you try this dish in one of the traditional trattorias in Firenze or—even better—when you will visit Impruneta. Pay attention, though: before ordering, ask about the ingredients. The original recipe doesn't have tomato sauce. The reason is simple: tomatoes entered italian cuisine only after 1492 (many years after Brunelleschi's death), as they were imported from America, the so-called "new world."

yourself, if you are navigating college with a tunnel vision mode toward graduation, if you are obsessed with your GPA or addicted to the classics, a semester abroad can be a moment of indulgence for yourself.

Firenze, and Florence in particular, can also offer an exposure to pop culture and mainstream trash attitudes: colorful markets full of yelling vendors can be a powerful source of inspiration. The same is true of other cliche destinations that the city can offer to your phone's camera. All of these can become memorable experiences, especially if you are a "nerdy", serious scholar. The cafes, the *panino* (sandwich) place, the "secret bakery"...and (why not?) even Space Electronic, the disco club that has served as the backdrop to the stereotyped "blast" night of so many international students in Firenze. But even there (almost deafened by pounding music and amidst wild dance moves) one can recognize traces of a past which is more recent and yet no less monumental.

Remember that stereotypes and prejudices exist because people make them exist.

It's not about what you do, it is about how you do it. Your mindset and your mood will make the difference.

Space Electronic is a nightclub in Firenze located on Via Palazzuolo, near the Santa Maria Novella train station. It was opened on February 27th, 1969, after refurbishing a mechanical workshop that had been abandoned as a consequence of the tragic 1966 flood.

In the 1970s, the Florentine discotheque we know today served as one of the most trendy venues of the Italian avant-gardes. A space for research and experimentation (assiduously frequented by such personalities as Dario Fo, Julian Beck and Judith Malina with their Living Theatre) it hosted concerts of such bands as the Van Der Graaf Generator, Rory Gallagher, Canned Heat, Equipe 84, Demetrio Stratos' Area and many more.

The design of the club was developed by Gruppo 9999, a collective of young architects who lived and worked in Firenze from 1968 to 1975. The founding members were Giorgio Birelli, Carlo Caldini, Fabrizio Fiumi and Paolo Galli.[23] Together with groups like ARCHIZOOM and SUPERSTUDIO, Gruppo 9999 contributed to the Florentine avant-garde movement later known as Architettura Radicale.

[23] In an interview published by the magazine Architectural Design, Carlo Caldini said: "We were very bad architects. We had no clients. We could not make a living out of our design capacities, so we built a discotheque to support ourselves ... The little money we made from that gave us the possibility to do whatever we wanted as architects."

The 1970s proved to be a fertile crisis: it was a period marked (both in Firenze and the rest of Italy) by strong political and social tensions, but also enriched by great desire for artistic and linguistic renewal.

"We must take better care of our planet!" was the prophetic slogan echoing in the rooms of what is now Space Electronic when the members of Gruppo 9999 were planting cabbages and other vegetables in the basement to install *"The Vegetable Garden House."*

Here is a passage from their manifesto, which was published for the 1972 Moma exhibition titled *Italy: The New Domestic Landscape*:

"RELAX. Immense energy cycles support our life within the Earth's very thin film. Our experience only depends on the forms of life, on the known and unknown phenomena that manifest themselves with the harmony and elegance of nature. Man and his environment are at the center of the research of the Gruppo 9999, whose projects express the fundamental hypothesis of a balance between scientific progress and nature. This happens thanks to a highly sophisticated technology, which—free from waste and pollution—operates to serve and protect both humankind and the environment."[24]

[24] Translated by the author from: F. Fiumi, P.Galli, G. Birelli e C. Caldini, *Ricordi di architettura/Architectural memoirs* (Firenze: Tipolitografia G.Capponi, 1972), 254.

Although barely recognizable today, the Space Electronic club is a piece of recent archeology, telling the story of one of the last moments when Firenze happened to be associated with the idea of "modernity." Today the club is usually packed with American students looking for entertainment, but already many years ago its walls bore the sign of cross stories joining Italy and the US.

After their graduation, Carlo Caldini and Mario Preti took a sort of 'study trip' across the American continent. This allowed their group to expand its architectural and cultural horizons by acquiring practical knowledge of the phenomena of the time, such as the Californian counterculture, Paolo Soleri's experiments in Arizona, the Montreal Expo of '67 and visits to metropolises like New York, Los Angeles, and Las Vegas.

The idea of opening a venue in Firenze with completely new features and functions came to Carlo Caldini and Fabrizio Fiumi, founders of Space Electronic, after seeing the Electric Circus, a disco in the Greenwich Village (New York) in December 1967.

At the Electric Circus, the visionary artist Rudi Stern was experimenting with Multimedia Art, a new form of art characterized by the coexistence and interaction of multiple languages (written texts, images, sounds, light effects, and animations) in the same medium. The one entered by Caldini and Fiumi was a large room with walls covered by projections: images, slides, film clips. and colored liquids. Live music and deejay sets alternated; the effect was a total involvement of music, images, and action. At the time Andy Warhol served as the Electric Circus art director and the Velvet Underground were the house band.

So, one of today's trashiest "must" of Florentine nightlife for students abroad was originally conceived by a group of students when they—too—were abroad.

Culture is fertile and has no borders.

After a few years of teaching US architecture students, one of them told me: "Franco, you keep telling us to lose ourselves in the city because the real city is between the monuments ... America is the same. You can't say you have been to our country if you keep visiting big cities like New York, Boston or Washington, DC" (At that time those were the only places in the US I had been to). "Next time you go to the US you must rent a car," he insisted, "and take a road trip, discovering the real dimensions and consistency of the country that one cannot grasp in the cities, especially big ones."

So, in 2009—during an academic trip for a couple of lectures (one in Boston at

Wentworth University and one in Alexandria, VA at the WAAC)—I overcame all the fears and dispelled all the doubts that traveling by car in a foreign country can trigger and rented a car. My plan was to travel all the way south from Boston (MA) to Alexandria (VA) passing through Rhode Island, Connecticut, New York, Pennsylvania, Maryland, and Washington, DC. I felt like I couldn't skip that test. I owed it to my students.

So I rented a Chevrolet Captiva at Logan Airport and, of course, I got immediately lost in the Boston freeway junctions. I hardly found my way to Connecticut between turnpikes and gas stations. I got honked at "right turn on red"—which I was not familiar with—and laughed at when I had a hard time putting gas in my car. Yet, those students were right: I experienced a completely different place and I recognized aspects of America that—until then—I had only seen in movies.

It is for this reason that, speaking of getting your hands dirty, when I saw the familiar shape of a motel (how many seminal movies are set in or around motels, from *Psycho* to *No Country for Old Men*) I couldn't resist. I stopped and stayed there for the night, making the night porter laugh (that time) and (later) my students too. Maybe it was not the most luxurious and clean room I've ever seen, but it certainly made my idea of the States sharper.

And it was much more authentic than a sightseeing bus tour of NYC.

14.

Context = Place - Space

In literature, context is the set of circumstances or the surrounding text that affects the meaning of a statement or a scene. Ignoring the context is one of the most common causes of misinterpretation.

Add Context! You are not designing in the middle of nothing.

–Franco Pisani, a random Desk Crit from the last 20 years

Context is about meaning, not language. Taking something out of context will completely change its meaning, even if keeping its readability. A plan, or an elevation, as well as a phrase can be orthographically and grammatically correct but completely misleading or wrong when considered in a given context.

Architects always act in context. Context is the origin and purpose of each project, not only the physical layout of the site where we are asked to design.

Context does not simply refer to the pre-existing buildings next to ours; rather, it is the pit, the matter, and the goal of architecture. Context exists before conception, during design and after construction. In other words, we can say that architecture is a never-ending series of modifications, which—one after the other—change the context.

This is the reason why it is of fundamental importance to add context to every architectural drawing and to realize that context has multiple (and not always tangible) dimensions. Quoting

Herman Melville: "It is not down in any map; true places never are."[25]

[25] Herman Melville, *Moby Dick, Or the Whale* (Boston: Northwestern U. Press, 1988) Ch.12, 98.

The very nature of the art of architecture is to serve humanity, its body and its soul. Even in its most spiritual form, it remains—in essence—an utilitarian art. Humans need places more than spaces. Context is the component that can fertilize spaces and make it possible for them to become places.

When we realize that context is the key to transform a space into a place, we discover that adding context is always a valid suggestion, not just abroad or in a strongly characterized situation.

So, why is this attitude more important abroad?

Because abroad it's easier to ask questions and more difficult to have "prefabricated" answers and misconceptions. From a book or a youtube tutorial, it's an easy step to swap a city like Firenze for the image of a series of monuments, thus seconding a cultural tradition that is attentive to recording qualitative emergencies, but uncertain in grasping the influences that context has on human activities.

When we live in a city for a significant period of time, we discover that its monuments are tied together by a complex and vital fabric. We find ourselves confused in formulating the diagnoses and the visions that are necessary to guide design activities in a world dominated by an ever-increasing number of factors.

Architecture is the simplest and more accessible form of art. At the same time, though, it's the most abstract and ephemeral of all.

To be an imaginative and creative architect, therefore, you must perform at many levels:, some are purely artistic and intellectual levels, others are scientific (technology, structure, materials, systems) and professional too (process, ethics, business).

So, we must ask ourselves the following question: What are the most suitable figurative models to represent context? Is it the pictorial model (fixing visual impressions), the geometric one (rendering spatial relations) or the literary one (evoking the most ineffable qualities)?

The answer is: one learns architecture by depicting it, drawing it, and telling it.

One of architecture's amazing virtues is that its context always varies, thus giving new meaning to the same "spatial envelope." Context can change the use of a building and yet preserve its spatial relevance. Look, for example, at Orsanmichele, an amazing building that has responded to contextual changing conditions and needs, always adapting its role and its program. Over the centuries, it has served as a vegetable garden, a loggia, a granary, the headquarters of the Florentine guilds, a church, and a museum (just to mention some of its many functions). Always different but always the same. The building saw contributions from different architects and builders, commissions from different patrons, and the work of amazing artists. In the end, its solid box shape still stands and features prominently in the skyline of Firenze.

Architects who are tied to context cannot do the same design twice, unless they only focus on superficial style.

Context always entails a physical component. However, focusing on a given context means giving the project qualities that are not exclusively physical and rigid, for they too move and change constantly. As such, they are difficult to represent in a technical drawing. The city is a living organism; within its unique and ever changing culture, new buildings act as the threads that weave the city's living traditions into a new and whole fabric. These threads are made of attitudes, materials, techniques, convenience, and intelligence more than superficial style.

Some visual and geometrical tools can prove helpful when dealing with a specific context's physical layout. I emphasize this in other chapters of this book, (especially BYOSB!, Let lines speak for you!, and How tall is a chair in centimeters?).

At the same time, dealing with the immaterial qualities of that same context means developing more sophisticated tools and a sensitivity that while abroad can (and must) be trained with a strong sense of commitment.

Once far from home habits, developing contextual sensitivity is both easier and necessary.

And don't forget: "Add context!"

15.

K.I.S.S.!

Don't worry! This suggestion has nothing to do with your social behaviours after studio. This suggestion is an acronym that speaks about a design engagement rule that can be best experienced and learned while abroad: "Keep It Simple and Straightforward!" but also: "Keep It Simple, Stupid!"

You don't have to be cool, to rule my world
Ain't no particular sign I'm more compatible with
I just want your extra time and your K.i.s.s.!
–Prince

Like all human affairs, architectural design should be ruled by the "law of parsimony" (Latin: *lex parsimoniae*) or by the so-called Occam's razor (Latin: *novacula Occami*), which is to say that entities should not be multiplied if there is no need for them:

Frustra fit per plura quod fieri potest per pauciora.
"It is useless to do with more what can be done with less."

As one of the most formative moments of my years at the school of architecture in Firenze, I vividly remember my studio professor—Gian Carlo Leoncilli Massi—commenting on my drawings during a desk crit: "You use a building crane to wear your jeans!"

Being so peculiar, a semester abroad is an opportunity to re-learn the basics of design. This way you won't make mistakes such as (metaphorically speaking) using a building crane for something that can be done with your hands. And this is true not only for design but also—and more importantly—for daily life too.

While abroad, you can discover that it's possible to live and have fun living in ways that are way more modest and essential than those you are used to. You can discover, for example, that owning a car (as well as other tools) is not always necessary to survive; sometimes a bicycle can do the job way better in an urban context. The same can be true of design tools. For instance, a laser cutter or a 3D printer are not always necessary to finalize a great design.

The world is showing a huge need for design in every field. If we reframe its boundaries, design is one of the tools that can impact and improve today's life conditions more than others. But this will happen only if we stop believing that design acts through heroic, extravagant, and ostentatious gestures.

Post Modernity is over!

Design must be an expression of intelligence and intelligence doesn't need visual claims to be appreciated. Lack of ornamentation and useless frills can be signs of spiritual strength. Intelligence requires the ability to listen. Knowing how to listen is not such a trivial quality; it requires attention and dedication.

The goal of design must be to defend humans from the elements by seconding nature not by opposing it. History teaches us that it is not possible to oppose nature's strength. Even if brought to their highest, our capacities are always incomparable to those of nature. Design must listen to nature and act by seconding it. Nature always shows intelligence in its acts and nature

always works by simplification and convenience...
How come soap bubbles are not cubic in shape?

Look for magic in the simplest gestures: respect the context, transform the obstructions imposed by the project into sparks for design, reduce the use of materials and colors, use the budget as a design tool, reuse everything you can reuse, repurpose what can be repurposed, understand how things are done.

Be sober and thrifty.

Don't try to be "too original"; don't overdo, don't overuse angles or weird shapes if there is no need for them, especially if you don't know the context in which you are acting. Re-discovering simplicity is one of the first steps toward a sustainable behaviour.

Make your project unique by understanding and tackling the design constraints and not by using "extravaganza."

A semester abroad in architecture is a moment when you can—at least for a small while—stop your design habits and re-learn the basics of your discipline.

To remove the unnecessary from your drawings, to go straight to the problem.

It's a semester in which you can pause your frenetic reality of production and finalization to start thinking about your architectural voice; to think about what and how you really want to design, to find ways to do it, and to decide what kind of life you want to lead.

Abroad you can find pleasure in being correct and complete, in valuing quality over quantity.

16.

How tall is a chair in centimeters?

An architecture studio must deal with space. And space is made of light, dimensions, and proportions.

Inevitably, there comes a moment in design when you need to shape something and…you can't do it without knowing its dimensions.

For American architecture students, spending a semester in Italy is—among many other things—an opportunity to cope with the metric system. How big is a door in centimeters? How tall is a chair? How wide is a bed? In the same way, students will learn—if they want—the weight of things in kilograms, the quantity of liquids or gasoline in liters and how cold a day is in Celsius degrees.

More importantly, they will discover that italians measure geographical distances in kilometers and not in hours.

New bizarre standards, new units, and a new language.

All of them should be seen not as obstacles but new tools that will strengthen the students' curriculum vitae, since Architecture is today a global discipline that involves different languages and standards. Being familiar with the metric system is an important skill to add to your CV, just like being fluent in different languages.

Although important and professionally relevant, understanding and using new units is not the only learning outcome of a semester abroad. The most important experience derived from the use of a set of different units and standards, is the fact that there is no right or wrong approach to reality, and reality is always very similar, independently of the unit system you place it in.

A chair is a chair, no matter what units you are using to measure it.

Always referring to reality is the key to understand the new system and become acquainted with it. I suggest that you take a tape meter with you (you can easily buy a cheap one for 99 cents in a convenience store and use it as a key chain) and measure everything you bump into, starting with stuff in your apartment. You will become "fluent" in the metric system sooner than you imagine.

Please don't try to discover some tricky formula to transform feet into meters and don't install any app on your phone to do so; this won't add either any skills to your profile or any confidence to your professional acting.

Measuring is necessary abroad, while you are practicing a new unit system, but it will prove a fruitful attitude also once you're back home.

Measuring is a basic component of the scientific method and, more importantly, a basic form of understanding the consistency of space, especially for architects.

The pit of architectural design is the built environment. In the near future, architects will focus mainly on contexts that are already built and contexts that have been encrusted with buildings.

The sheets on which architects work are not blank; they are used sheets that we must reuse. They are filled with lines; some are ink lines, some pencil lines, some lines have been already deleted and they are barely visible, while others left vivid marks on the paper. They must all be considered carefully.

Knowing exactly the consistency of the built environment (in other words, surveying it) is crucial for successful design.

As of today, there is no sector of human activity (starting with constructions) that does not show alarming signs that the planet is about to reach its "limits."

The built environment is a field where limits have become evident only in fairly recent times. The awareness of how much the territory is a non-renewable asset is dramatically topical. It is thus fundamental to know its consistency, current health, and evolutionary dynamics.

The necessity of surveying scientifically and understanding with precision the state of the art of the built environment was already clear in a letter from Baldassarre Castiglione and Raphael to Pope Leone X dating from 1519.[26] In it these two famous figures (a writer and a painter) suggested that the Pope promote and support a survey campaign to measure and report the state of the antique monuments in the city of Rome. The survey drawings, which Raphael described in that document, should have been carried out rigorously, using a scientific method in plan, section (the interior) and elevation (the exterior with its decorative apparatus). "Since," as Raphael explains, "the way of drawing specific to the architect is different from that of the painter, I shall say what I think opportune so that all the measurements can be understood and all the members of the buildings can be determined without error."[27] It appears clear in this letter that survey drawings are important today (as they were back then) for two main reasons: first, to protect and preserve the majesty of the monuments; second, to

[26] The "Lettera di Raffaello a Leone X," 1519, was actually written by Baldassare Castiglione for the artist and it constitutes the founding document of the protection and conservation of Italy's historic and artistic heritage.

[27] "Lettera di Raffaello a Leone X", 1519 (Munich, Bayerische Staatsbibliothek, cod. it. 37b) in Francesco P. Di Teodoro, Raffaello, Baldassar Castiglione e la 'Lettera a Leone X' (Bologna: Nuova Alfa Editoriale, 1994): 115-27; translated as "The Letter to Leo X by Raphael and Baldassarre Castiglione, c.1519," in Vaughan Hart and Peter Hicks, Palladio's Rome: A Translation of Andrea Palladio's Two Guidebooks to Rome (New Haven: Yale University Press, 2006): 179-92.

learn—in the process—methods both to design those objects and interact with them.

So, the survey that Castiglione and Rapahel wanted to conduct was meant both as a way of knowing the built environment and finding inspiration to design.

The fine line between drawing to register data (survey drawing) on the one hand and drawing to conceive new ideas (project drawing) on the other is at once feeble and unstable.

The fact is, any architectural drawing is a codified interpretation of reality. At the same time, it's a privileged tool to understand the existing environment and to predict the future. The very act of surveying is affected by the cultural assumptions influencing the critical collection of data. Likewise, design is influenced by the culture that generated it. Eyes only see what the brain understands. As an example, we can think of the *Cupolone*, the majestic symbol that for almost six centueies now has characterized the skyline of Firenze. Filippo Brunelleschi built it on top of the drum of the Santa Maria del Fiore cathedral using techniques that are still not completely clear today. The geometry of both the drum and the subsequent dome is based on an irregular octagon, displaying discrepancies as significant as 60 cm among its eight sides.

Nobody knows if this is simply an error caused by building techniques or an intentional act of pious humility, as perfection can only be referred to God.

Although we can easily detect these discrepancies even without sophisticated tools, centuries have gone by without any surveys of the dome noticing them.

Which drawing is more correct to represent the dome?

The irregular one (i.e., faithful to the material layout of the construction) or the idealized one (i.e., faithful to the geometric scheme)?

We survey, and then we design what?

The body or the idea?

The act of surveying a building demands thoughtful observation. To see a space means always "to perform an abstraction because seeing consists in the grasping of structural features rather than in the indiscriminate recording of details."[28]

[28] Rudolph Arnheim, *Visual Thinking* (Berkeley, University of California Press, 1997), 68.

[29] Andrea Palladio, *Schizzi Vari di queste Terme* (London, RIBA Library Drawings Collection) Vol.VII, Folio 6/r+v.

There is a famous and intriguing series of drawings by Palladio—now at the RIBA archive—that survey the remains of the ancient Baths of Agrippa (Latin: Thermae Agrippae) in Rome.

In those drawings[29] the architect investigates and dreams up how they should have looked at the time of Nero. I like to think (and I believe that in doing so I'm not so far from reality) that in those same years Palladio was already thinking about the design of his Venetian churches: San Giorgio Maggiore and Il Redentore.

By measuring, proportioning, disassembling, and reassembling the plan of the Baths, the pages of his sketchbook became an incubator for spatial ideas. Thought started as the representation of a monument through the survey of its relics, that page gradually became the design (probably even the project) of another building.

Surveying is already designing, today more than ever.

17.

Drop it (the stereotype) like it's hot.

Stereotypes exist (and we all know what we are speaking of when we speak of stereotyped college students).

This is particularly true while abroad, where language barriers sometimes act as noise in the understanding of things and episodes, stereotypes often become lifebuoys to skip decisions.

The experience of studying abroad is losing its original meaning because of the standardization of expectations. The to do lists filled by the students before departure are shared on social media and copied by most. It thus happens that the whole experience ends up being completely standardized and stereotyped as regards both expectations and accomplishments.

According to Hannah Arendt, the city is where you can experience the unexpected. In the near future, architects will work mainly (if not exclusively) in cities, as the world population is quickly and inexorably becoming urban.

Urban areas are the diverse, complex, intensely developed and decisive media in which we, as humans, are confronted with the global challenge of how to interact more harmoniously (locally and effectively) with the rest of the natural world. Being abroad, living for a semester in a

'This is a battle, boys,' he cried. 'War! You are souls at a critical juncture. Either you will succumb to the will of academic -hoi polloi-, and the fruit will die on the vine—or you will triumph as individuals.'
–N.H. Kleinbaum, *Dead Poets Society*

real city, is a challenge for every student to make a difference if he or she takes the road less traveled by (as Robert Frost put it).[30]

This piece of advice will be helpful in regard to both personal daily life and professional training.

In a design studio you don't have to entertain people; you are not performing alone on the stage of your project to the benefit of your teachers or for the records. Instead, you are learning design and you are doing it for yourself (or, at least, for your portfolio).

[30] "Two roads diverged in a wood, and I—I took the one less traveled by, And that has made all the difference." –Robert Frost, *The Road Not Taken*, 1916.

In my twofold—or split—professional life (both as an architect and as an architectural educator) I have often looked at portfolios either to hire interns for my office or to advise former students.

I don't know if it is because of the typical production mode of digital drawings or because of the standardization of taste and expectations produced by internet globalization, but most portfolios look the same, both in content and form. Usually the pages and the projects that arouse interest are those developed outside the regular curriculum or during peculiar experiences, like a semester abroad (no matter where it took place). These pages deserve appreciation because of their originality; they stand out thanks to their diversity. They are different (neither better nor worse) than the others: just different because they were born under different circumstances.

In a world still dominated by the unceasing search for formal novelty, many architects continue to pursue "being new" as their prime objective, transplanting forms from product design, fashion, statistical analysis and other disciplines. Technological improvement has made anything possible. Anything goes, even if it's not necessary, justified or understood.

The weird and contradictory result of this apparent anarchy of expression is an incredible homologation of products, the impoverishment of the imagination, and a loss of personality for Architects and Designers. Usually digital renderings speak more of the software that produced them than of the designer who conceived them.

A nice drawing, carefully crafted, simple and effective, showing an understanding of spatial issues, still works to inspire curiosity and show commitment and skills. To be different in the chaos of "standardized extravaganza" means to go back to basics, to the possibility for a slower, smaller, and more careful production, where meaning, work ethic, convenience, and construction merge together into a new aesthetic.

Quoting Adolf Loos again: "Don't be afraid of being called unmodern. Changes in the old methods of construction are only allowed if they can claim to bring improvement, otherwise stick with the old ways. Because the truth, even if hundreds of years old, has more inner connection than falsehood, which walks beside us."[31]

[31] Loos, Adolf; Adolf Opel, *Ornament and Crime: Selected Essays.* (Riverside, CA: Ariadne Press 1997), 69.

Being different doesn't mean being original or eccentric; it means being authentic and critical of conventions. Radical developments have never emerged from a blank slate condition (some sort of tabula rasa). Innovators in architecture—from Palladio to Le Corbusier, from Brunelleschi to Koolhaas—have always worked in close contact with architecture culture, all the while displaying a fearless capacity for being different.

The idea of Architects as extravagant geniuses dressed in black who express themselves through bizarre formal inventions is just hilarious and a bit outdated. It may only work (at best) in a movie plot.

Today—more than ever—architects must be brave and able to question habits and conventions, splitting formal issues from spatial smartness.

The disciplinary boundaries of Architecture are changing quickly, as fast as many important changes occurring in today's society.

In a sort of retrofit, architects are becoming once again a liaison between clients, developers and users. Vitruvius already said this more almost 2,000 years ago. Architects must possess multifaceted skills in order to interface different, sometimes very specific know-hows. The physical form of the built environment is not their main goal. Their skills must involve support in decision making, critical development of implicit programs, and counseling for the actors who transform the built environment.

It goes without saying that practicing diversity is easier and less demanding for a student when he or she is abroad than at home; it just comes naturally.

When abroad, we all are strangers: even if we don't want to, we act in a different way.

18.

Tell it to … !

Architecture is a form of art that deals with other's needs and sensitivities.

Learning to transform a critique into a productive germ is an attitude that must be trained in school. One day you will discuss projects with your clients just like today you are discussing them with teachers, listening to critical observations and responding. Even if your original idea has been partially altered by your teacher's suggestions, the design at the end will be your own design. To be fully satisfied by it you need to develop the ability to step back and look at it in its entirety from a distance.

Exposing yourselves to criticism and listening to people's comments without taking offense will test the motivation of your design positions. More importantly, it will make you capable of describing your designs, explaining them, and sharing your decisions with your interlocutors.

Usually a bad reception is the result of a badly told story.

The romantic idea of the architect who lives isolated in an ivory tower of creativity, unable to speak to others and to communicate architecture with simple words is outdated and obsolete. Even

We need very strong ears to hear ourselves judged frankly, and because there are few who can endure frank criticism without being stung by it, those who venture to criticize us perform a remarkable act of friendship, for to undertake to wound or offend a man for his own good is to have a healthy love for him.

–Michel de Montaigne

when common, it didn't help architecture at all. If architecture today is not considered as it should, it is also because architects stopped speaking of architecture in a way that the rest of the world could understand.

Among other things, drawing can be a form of storytelling.

Reading, understanding, and criticizing architecture is a training routine to find ways to support and motivate all your decisions, and to restart to tell the story of the contribution of design to the built environment. To appreciate your work, people must understand it.

Let's just think of the tale reported by Vitruvius to explain the birth of the Corinthian capital[32]: a wicker basket (*kalathos* in Greek) bearing funeral offerings, was conveyed to the grave of a deceased beautiful young girl near Corinthus. It was placed on the tomb and covered with a roof tile to protect all the objects that had been dear to the girl in her lifetime. The basket happened to rest on top of an acanthus root, thus causing the acanthus leaves to spread around it and curl over in volutes at the sides. Seeing this, the sculptor Kallimachos (who, Vitruvius points out, was given the name *katatechnos* by the Athenians for the elegance and refinement of his marble carving) created a column based on this model.

[32] G. Morolli, *L'architettura di Vitruvio: una guida illustrata,* (Firenze: Alinea,1988), 35.

Fiction or fact? Nobody knows, but Vitruvius wrote more or less 350 years after the supposed facts. One is thus led to believe that there must be a good deal of fiction in this account. Whatever the case, what I consider interesting is that Vitruvius found a narrative way to tell the story (fictional or not) and to explain why the Corinthian capital has that peculiar shape.

In my studios the word "cool" is banned. Students can't use it when speaking of architecture. There are two main reasons for this. First, I don't believe in "cool architects" (when this means being snobbish and distant from people in reality). Second, the word "cool" is foggy and it can suggest (maybe even cause) laziness. A building is not cool; it can be intriguing, amazing, appealing, glamorous, depressing, or dark, but not cool.

In addition to *cool* students are not allowed to use formulas like *kind of*, *sort of*.

Apart from being vague, these expressions are too connected to certain peculiar socio-cultural contexts. As such, they generate misunderstandings in an architecture class.

I ask my students to avoid those words because architects must use precise words to describe or criticize the outcome of their work. Design will be (somehow, someday) their job and—I hope—

their source of income. In this endeavor, laziness will not do. It also won't contribute positively to your projects presentations.

It may sound pretentious for an Italian architect to pass judgement on English words and idioms, especially with students who are native English speakers. If I make this impression, I'm sorry and I hope you accept my apologies. Maybe, though, my being less used to the rhythm and the musicality of the English language puts me in a better position to spot abuses and unnecessary iterations in wording.

This said, here is my next recommendation to architecture students: participate and listen carefully to critics and presentations, answer questions about your design decisions, and never get offended by comments. Comments made at studio presentations are not about your personality: they are about your design. Architectural designs are not crystals and perfect gems.

In architecture there is no copyright; nobody can copyright a building. Living in a foreign city will make this "crystal" clear.

Places like Italy (and Firenze in particular) can teach you this. Architecture is a contribution to a choral, lively and neverending piece called "the built environment." There is no final definitive layout for it. So, architects shouldn't worship authorship.

On this, I would like to take the Ponte Vecchio as a case study.

One of the most famous symbols of Firenze, the Old Bridge is known worldwide as one of the most famous masterpieces in this city. Let's walk to Ponte Santa Trinita and take a nice picture of the Ponte Vecchio. Maps of georeferenced pictures of the city show that this is one of the places where most photos are taken. The reason is quite simple: this spot offers two great sights at once. The next bridge after Ponte Vecchio following the stream of the river Arno, Santa Trinita offers beautiful sunsets nearly every day on one side and a perfect, straight view of the west elevation of Ponte Vecchio on the other. As such, it stands out as an astonishing view in all light and weather conditions, a coveted prey for tourists and instagrammers. Let's take this stereotyped picture and focus for a while on what we get in it.

The first question that springs to mind is: Who did it? What's the name of the "author"?

The main stone structures of the bridge (basically, the three segmental arches and two *pietraforte* pillars supporting them) date back to 1345. In that year, Taddeo Gaddi—one Giotto's pupils—designed and built those structures, as the previous ones had been severely damaged by a series of floods (the one that occurred in 1333 proving particularly violent and destructive). At least this is what Giorgio Vasari reported in his *Lives of the Most Excellent Painters, Sculptors, and Architects* 200 years after the "new" Ponte Vecchio was built.

The segmental arches (a rather unusual solution at the time) made it possible to cover the span between the two banks with only two pillars without causing an excessive rise. Also, this made it easier for people to circulate on the bridge and reduced the number of potential obstacles to the current in the event of a new flood.

Good job, Taddeo!

The small constructions on the two sides of the main street running on the bridge were built in 1442 to host the butchers of Firenze. That year, the Bargello (a military authority in charge of keeping peace and justice in town) forced all local butchers to set up their shops in this location, in hopes of reducing the foul smell caused by the butchering leftovers. On the bridge, butchers could use the river Arno as a natural sewage system.

From that moment on, to extend the area that shops could cover, cantilevered rooms were added to the original structure with different shapes and dimensions. In 1565, Giorgio Vasari (then serving the Grand Duke Cosimo I de' Medici as architect in charge of building the Uffizi) was asked to design an enclosed passageway to link Palazzo Vecchio—the government building— to the Medici residence in Palazzo Pitti, on the other side of the river. Having suppressed the Republic of Florence, Cosimo I felt insecure and unsafe in public. Besides, the Florentines had always had a love-hate relationship with the Medici family.

Vasari knew that the construction of a new bridge would cost too much. So, he decided to use the existing bridge structure to cross the Arno and passing over the butchers' shops. Only one local family—the Mannellis—opposed this project, as it would demolish their medieval tower on the southern end of the bridge. As a solution, Vasari designed his Corridor in such a way as to bypass the tower and leave it intact. Still today the Torre de' Mannelli is a major feature in the profile of both the bridge and Vasari's elevated addition to it.

As for the butchers, in 1593 (almost 40 years after Vasari finished his Corridor) Ferdinando I (the son of Cosimo I) replaced their bad smelling shops with the much more elegant goldsmith shops that we can still see on the bridge today.

Also, a new series of updates to the small buildings started to take place, thus changing once again the elevation of this monument.

In 1860, when Vittorio Emanuele II (King of Italy) visited Firenze for the first time, the corridor (and, consequently, the bridge) was modified by opening three large windows on the west side. This made it possible, from then on, to enjoy a beautiful view of the sunset from inside the corridor. On that specific occasion, it also offered King Vittorio Emanuele the opportunity to watch from a privileged position the firework show that had been specially organized for him.

Throught that window on the Arno, sunsets were also enjoyed by Hitler, Mussolini, and some of the highest Nazi and Fascist representatives on the occasion of the Führer's trip to Italy in May 1938. When the German troops left the city at the end of World War II, this was the only bridge in Florence that they did not blow up.

According to one of the stories on how the Ponte Vecchio was saved from destruction, some Florentine goldsmiths sabotaged the bombs that the Nazi troups had placed there. What is known for sure is that shortly before the end of World War II—during the so-called Battle of Florence—the areas around the bridge (especailly, Por Santa Maria, Via Guicciardini and Borgo San Jacopo), were heavily damaged.[33] The mainly residential buildings on the left and right banks of the river (which are evidently more recent than the others) were hastily built in the early 1950, causing harsh polemics among architects, politicians, art historians and the Florentines themselves.

[33] This is hard to imagine as of today. For this reason I strongly suggest the vision of the fourth Episode of the neorealist movie Paisan by Roberto Rossellini, 1946 filmed in this area just after the end of World War Two.

Last but not least, going back to our picture, let's take a look at the people moving back and forth in the small piazza right halfway through the bridge. You can find them there at any time of the day, any day of the year. They too are contemporary, actual actors who can transform each one of our pictures into unique pieces.

Who is the "author" that can sign it all?

But also and more importantly: "Does it really matter?"

19.

Be good! Stop yakking about sustainability.

It's a matter of design! As designers, we often project ourselves into the future because we design things that will come to fruition in the future. For this reason, optimism should inform our professional lives. All the more so, we shouldn't accept the derogatory notion that poorly designed, dishonorable, destructive systems are all we can do. This kind of "deficit thinking" would lead us to believe that the best thing we can do is try not to be so bad.

Humans are not born "bad"; they may become bad when they live in altered and unnatural systems of values, without either hopes or dreams.

Some twenty years ago Braungart and McDonough wrote an interesting book titled *Cradle to Cradle: Remaking the Way We Make Things.*[34] In it, among other things, they ask designers to quit the idea that "being less bad" is the best goal they can attain and—as such—the only potential improvement in their field.

[34] William McDonough, Michael Braungart, *Cradle to Cradle: Remaking the Way We Make Things.* (New York: North Point Press, 2002).

This "be less bad" approach ultimately leads to a lack in imagination.

Is there a way to at least try to be 100% good?

Sometimes aiming to be completely good can result in a truly revolutionary approach. Marginal gains are only important when you completely accept the rules of the game (even when they are proved wrong). As of today, reformulating the question completely is better than providing yet another answer to it. It involves bravery and courage, but these two qualities have always been the foundations of design.

I don't believe in a sustainable kind of architecture within an unsustainable context.

In fact, I don't believe in sustainable architecture.

"Sustainable Architecture" shouldn't exist, because by accepting the possibility of a "Sustainable Architecture" we accept the possibility of an "Un-Sustainable Architecture."

Architecture—by any means—is, and can only be, sustainable.

There is good architecture and bad architecture. The latter is a contradiction in terms, because bad architecture is not architecture. Besides, bad architecture tends not to last, as nature rejects it.

I literally go crazy when students tell me that they have an interest in sustainable architecture, maybe wearing flip-flops and shorts in January as they say so.

Sustainability can't be an option, a mere formula to add something modern, hi-tech, and expensive to design. I find this approach obsolete, uninteresting and—basically—stupid.

It often happens that sustainability issues are misunderstood by pairing them with technical matters, hi-tech materials and related solutions. Living for a semester in a historic city can serve as a lesson to learn how, in the past (when the word "sustainability," far from being as fashionable as today, did not even exist yet), human life was actually more sustainable than now.

Most apartments in Firenze do not have air conditioning. I often hear students complain about this, especially in the early Fall Semester, as summer is pretty hot here. It sounds as if they couldn't survive without air conditioning. Meanwhile, they seem not to know how pleasant and comfortable shaded rooms can be. More importantly, they have not been taught (apparently) that opening and closing both windows and shutters at different times of the day can significantly improve the temperature and the quality of the air (especially if done on a regular basis).

Have you ever stood in front of an air conditioning unit in mid-summer? I mean the outdoor unit that is usually placed on the sidewalk close to the shop door? When you stand in front of it, the heat is unbearable: the outside temperature is high because of the season and to keep a lower temperature inside a room we increase the outside temperature even more.

Basically, to defend ourselves from an enemy, we make it stronger. Although insane and completely irrational, this "strategy" is widely accepted.

Is there a way we can make this sustainable?

A traditional mid-size italian town is a sustainable, vibrant human settlement that provides all citizens with ample opportunities to lead a most decent life in harmony with the natural environment.

The idea that sees the city as opposed to nature is not only superficial but false and dangerous, too. The city has always been the expression of a balance between natural and artificial; its boundaries (be they either thick urban walls or the citizens' intangible identities) have always served as permeable membranes to keep this equilibrium fertile.

Humanity today must face the challenge of averting further ecological damage by reducing the use of natural resources and stopping environmental deterioration. Instead of big cities for a small planet[35], what we need are small cities for a bigger planet.

Not sprawling of small private properties but systems of integrated mutual conveniences.

[35] Richard Rogers, *Cities for a Small Planet*, (Roma: Erid'A/Kappa, 1997).

There is not a single acre of natural land that is worth anthropization or transformation into a building. Within this framework, Architecture is going back to its origins, that is, being the art of creating spaces rather than buildings. As of today, creating space has more to do with making room than making buildings.

Like in many Italian cities, the past is still clearly visible in Firenze and the built environment coexists with the non-human world. A semester abroad is the opportunity to experience and discover that we can survive and be happy without a car, that walking is not a sport but the natural way for humans to move around, that wearing shorts, t-shirt and flip-flops in January is not a sign of progress but simply a stupid, epic failure.

20.

Enjoy! And get into the swing.

Your semester abroad is going to be a game changer, whether you like it or not.

Tu proverai sì come sa di sale lo pane altrui [36]

–Dante

This is true not only because of the amount of posts on social media that will make you brag about this transformative experience, but also (and more importantly) because you have been living in those pictures for four months.

Among other things, while in Firenze for a whole semester you tried Florentine bread, which is notoriously saltless.

Also, you must have felt the freezing *tramontana* (north-western wind) in November or the *bollore* (scorching heat) of a summer day.

When I started to teach students from Marywood University, as one of the many agreements that an institutional partnership requires, I promised Greg Hunt (the then Dean of the School of Architecture) that I would take his students to see Palladio and Scarpa in the Veneto every single semester. So, whenever possible, after the break I organize a long weekend in that part of Italy to see places like the Brion Cemetery, Castelvecchio, Villa Rotonda, and the Teatro Olimpico.

And each time we approach the incredible interior-exterior space of the Teatro, I repeat this experiment:

[36] "Thou shalt prove how salt the savour is of other's bread"
–Dante Alighieri, *The Divine Comedy of Dante Alighieri: Hell, Purgatory, Paradise*, translated by Henry F. Cary, (New York: P.F. Collier & Son, 1909),Pd, XVII, l. 57-58.

I blindfold a couple of students with my scarf and I guide them inside the wooden cavea.

Most of my students are familiar with the phenomenal Palladian theater from pictures they have seen in History of Architecture classes or from books.

Once inside, I remove the blindfold from their eyes. The result is always the same: flabbergasted faces and lots of "Wow!"

Although social media are doing their best to dominate and dictate our lives, there is still a huge difference between sitting on the steps of the Teatro Olimpico or watching a Youtube video about it.

Architecture is a highly demanding and ungrateful discipline.

It requires many sacrifices and a never-ending apprenticeship, all of which are seldom balanced by an adequate salary. For sure, there are nine to five jobs that pay way better. As an architect, you'll often bring your job home with you; sometimes, it won't let you go home at all, and it will certainly deprive you of hours of sleep.

The only possibility to make it worth is to learn to appreciate and enjoy design in every bit, to learn to be eager to see the results of your excitement in a drawing or in a model. In other words, to find magic in designing; without that, it will be hard to enjoy being an Architect.

So, while abroad, start to get into the swing!

Sometimes people say architects are boring because we tend to put architecture in everything we do. Actually, I think they are simply envious; they don't love their job as much as we love ours.

There is a big difference between a nerd and a slacker, between a loser and an influencer.

Someone who is seriously enjoying his or her job is just smart.

If we look at the words "enjoyment" and *divertimento* (the latter being one of the former's possible Italian translations) from an etymological point of view, we discover a couple of interesting things that pertain to studying abroad.

The word *divertimento* comes from the Latin *de-vertire*, which means go or turn elsewhere (like a detour, so to speak). It suggests that we only have fun or enjoy ourselves when we do things that differ from our usual routines. Abroad is elsewhere, not only spatially but also—and more importantly—from a cultural point of view.

Being abroad is everything but a routine, as we said before; it won't happen every semester.

Fun and curiosity should go hand in hand. On the contrary, today's youths are scared by unknown contexts and they feel pressured to succeed. This is largely due to their worshipping achievement in ways that previous generations did not know. Among the lessons we can learn while abroad is that the unknown is challenging, not scary; it's exciting, not anxiogenic.

A dreary world where competition is based on cunning and prevarication at the expense of competence and knowledge is doomed to become poorer and, eventually, not competitive at all.

Far from being a joke, to have fun and enjoy life is one of the most serious things we can do in this world.

The verb "to enjoy" derives from Old French *enjoer*, which means to give joy or to receive with joy, to take delight in. Honestly, I prefer to flip the usual claim "There is no pleasure where there is duty" into "There is no duty where there is pleasure."

Is it possible to combine joy, pleasure, and delight with work?

Luckily enough, Architecture offers this possibility more than other disciplines. Yet one must learn to have fun designing. How can a semester abroad help us to learn to enjoy working?

To answer this last question we need to investigate the meaning and the components of finding pleasure and having fun.

When do we experience serious fun and enjoyment?

Fun, as I said, is not passive entertainment. Awareness is the first component of fun. We really have fun when we are present in time, space, body, and spirit. Some psychologists call this status "flow," when you are so involved in what you are doing that you lose track of time and place; everything happens naturally, although what is being done is actually very demanding. Design can trigger this status and design abroad even more so.

A semester abroad is not a duty, as it is not mandatory; it can be strongly suggested, but it won't be imposed on you. Students decide to go abroad choosing among the different options offered by their home institution. Some schools offer a single destination as a legacy, some offer alternative options in different locations. Whatever the case, going abroad is usually a pondered decision, although expectations will eventually materialize only to a limited extent or not at all. Students must plan their semester abroad in advance, get their visas and find money (at least for the flight).

The second component is participation in Beauty, I mean that Beauty which doesn't depend on taste and compromises, but only on deep simplicity, clean gestures, and essential forms.

We have fun when we feel we are contributing to something bigger than us. Design should be about Beauty, and this is particularly true when one is abroad.

There is no doubt Greece has been one of the cradles of architecture. It may also be true that having a blast wearing a pink toga in synthetic silk at the Pink Palace in Corfu could trigger a certain "flow." Yet, I don't think it has much to do with joy, delight, good taste and—more importantly—with Beauty.

It doesn't happen naturally and it ends up with a huge headache. It is neither about curiosity and experience nor about authenticity and sense of place.

It is just ugly and goofy.

A semester abroad is also an opportunity to start to enjoy your job as an architect, to start to value design in all its peculiarities, to get into the swing or to decide to step back from it. When you are in Firenze you can start to appreciate architecture 24/7, inside and outside studio. If this attempt fails and you don't find it stimulating, then maybe in the trip to Greece scheduled for next weekend you will prefer the Pink Palace to the Parthenon.

Well, no big deal. I hope you will have the time of your life, filled with all the fun and the entertainment promised by "The Hidden

[37] Vance Packard, *The Hidden Persuaders*, (Philadelphia: D.McKay Company,1957).

Persuaders"[37] who suggested it to you!

It's your decision. It's a decision that—I hope—you will take consciously and sincerely.

Design itself is about making decisions, addressing the future, and excluding possibilities. Sometimes successfully, sometimes not.

I defined the semester abroad as a game-changer in the first line of this chapter. This is true also in the sense that a semester abroad can become a mirror to observe yourself in a different context. This reflection (in both its meanings: as an image but also as a form of meditation) can stimulate your determination and your will to pursue a career in architecture or, on the other hand, it can serve as a deterrent to it.

But instead of discovering this after graduation, you can find out after your semester abroad, when you can still change your major and do so to your advantage.

THX.

Acknowledgments.

I started teaching architecture to American students, almost by accident, nearly without realizing it. During my first semester I remember

very well, given my weird spoken English, the difficulties in finding simpler and more incisive forms of expression than those I was used to.

Since that first semester I have experienced a continuous intertwining of things taught and things learned, because teaching is a form of learning. A continuous enrichment.

Also by accident, (since I would never have imagined myself writing a book) I started writing these pages. Taking advantage of the days emptied by the pandemic, I began to gather all the thoughts generated, by the interaction with students. I took the opportunity offered by the forced inactivity to arrange and organize at least some of those programs and topics that have remained unattended to over the years for lack of time and focus.

Within a lockdown, from March to May 2020, thoughts and memories branched out one after the other and the number of pages grew. The notes became a book.

A book, like the results of a design studio, is always a collective work. Even if signed by a single author those responsible are many and the voices overlap and merge consistently.

So, in these years, students became masters, teachers became recipients, friends became an inspiration, colleagues became friends, enemies became allies, uncomfortable adventures became stimuli, academic needs became educational opportunities.

I would like to dedicate a toast of thanks to all those who played a role in this adventure:

to all those people who have enriched me and with whom I have shared beliefs and doubts (even the most unpleasant and inconvenient ones);

to all the teachers I have met (particularly those who will not be able to read these pages but who are constantly inspiring me);

to the students I have met in these twenty years but also to those I hope I will continue to meet every beginning of the semester. You are mirrors capable of continuously challenging and stimulating me;

to Francisco Sanin of SUF, whom I am grateful for introducing me to the mentality of American students;

to Luis Carranza and Roberto Viola, both of whom I met in the summer of 2009 at RWU, who have since then become recurring icons on my WhatsApp;

to Mike Crosbie who always appreciated my prose;

to Maurizio Sabini for the encouragement and the consideration;

to Emilia Daniele, Stefano Corazzini, Simone Barbi, Marco Brizzi and Paola Giaconia, for the dialogues;

to James Eckler and Jim Sullivan and all the crew at MUSoA;

to Marco Frascari, who I have not been able to meet in person but who continues to live in all those who have been fascinated by his personality and his world. Among these I would like to thank for being a partner in crime Alessandro Ayuso, who has stepped up from his former role as a student to that of a colleague.

Finally, a very special toast (but also some extra drinks) goes to:

Stefano Baldassarri, for the wisdom with which he tamed my naive and creative English and made it more suitable for the pages of a book.

Igor Marjanović and Jonathan Foote, who I stumbled upon on the tortuous path of architectural education. First friends of friends, then friends in architecture, now Friends: they helped me define and encouraged me to finish this book.

Alicia Moreira for her help in making these pages look lighter and more elegant.

Raffa, EmmaValme and Zeno, life and quarantine mates, whom I had to leave at home too often in order to cultivate my American experiences. The pride and love you feel while having breakfast together every morning is better than anything I can express in words. On the count of three: FAMILY! 1…2…3…

B.
Beyond Bagging Buildings.

An Afterword by Jonathan Foote

Jonathan Foote, Ph.D, is an architect (MAA) and Associate Professor at Aarhus School of Architecture, Denmark. His teaching, editorial work and research focuses on the architectural translation between ideas, drawings and materials. He has published on the drawings and workshop practices of Michelangelo Buonarroti and Francesco Borromini, and he is currently editing a forthcoming book on Sigurd Lewerentz.

Traveling abroad for architecture students is often likened to the nineteenth century Grand Tour. By this comparison, study abroad is a tradition whereby young travelers absorb the work of the great masters of Italy, transforming themselves in the process from students of architecture into learned and connected professionals. The mythology of the Grand Tour is no doubt the basis on which many study and travel abroad programs are based today. Thus, each new generation of architecture students seems to have a responsibility, to the extent of their means, to make a ritualized "return" to the origins of western architecture to experience and revalidate the architectural canon, both contemporary and historical.

In today's increasingly inter-connected and complex world, however, the notion that a single canon exists for the architecture student is more tenuous than ever. The transformational basis of study abroad must therefore justify itself beyond the proverbial Grand Tour as sum of visiting important buildings curated by an architecture professor— what a former colleague once joked as "bagging buildings." The idea of stuffing buildings into one's travel bag is a humorous take on the nagging legacy of the Grand Tour, where the goal is to collect some canonical examples that can be uncritically absorbed into one's personal design language. If history is to be our teacher, however, it might behoove us to take a slightly different point of departure. For this I refer the reader to the famous 'study abroad' taken by Filippo Brunelleschi and Donatello from Firenze to Roma in the early 1400s.

The trip is remembered on account of Antonio Manetti's Vita di Filippo Brunelleschi, and it was later repeated and elaborated upon by Giorgio Vasari in his own biographies of Brunelleschi in 1550 and 1568. Filippo was in his mid-twenties when he departed Firenze for Roma, which in those days was a five- or six-day journey by horseback. Together with Donatello, they sought to study ancient architecture and sculpture, although it was not exactly clear what kind of knowledge would emerge from such a project. Roma at this time was a squalid and chaotic place, having shrunk from a city of over one million at the height of the Republic to less than twenty thousand in 1400. Clues to an ancient glory were abound, but after enduring nearly a millennium of abuse and neglect, the city's greatest secrets had succumbed to untold layers of mud, broken bricks, and stone fragments. Thus, the duo would spend their days primarily as excavators, an act that earned them the notoriety of the locals, who reasoned they were either looking for buried treasure or, worse, re-enacting pagan rituals of predicting the future through geomancy. Although, by our standards today, a trip from Firenze to Roma would hardly count as "abroad," the conditions are similar: the travelers found themselves cast into a foreign urban setting, having to live by their wits in a place characterized by a strange language and inexplicable customs.

Brunelleschi brought tools with him for measuring. He measured and surveyed details, elements, and even entire buildings. He created his own secret notational system of recording his findings to the bafflement of his travel companion. Not only were they mocked and estranged by the locals, they had problems with money and lived like paupers. Donatello returned to Firenze early, but Brunelleschi stayed on and off in Roma for several years, it seems. Vasari recounts that Filippo took no interest in eating or sleeping, as he was singularly focused on uncovering the architectural secrets of the past. He dug into mud of the Roman fora, crawled onto the roof of the Pantheon, and intently pinned his measuring compass on practically any architectural detail he could find.

Traveling to Roma at the time was common for religious pilgrims, but nobody imagined the city as a source for excavating knowledge from the pagan, ruinous landscape. Brunelleschi's trip thus represented an entirely new kind of journey—a secular "pilgrimage" that brings about a personal transformation through knowledge gathering and purposeful otherness. In this way, although Brunelleschi ostensibly traveled to Roma to "bag" some architecture, the conditions by which he worked indicated a much more broad and abundant learning process. Unlike the travelers of the Grand Tour, the sites and experiences were not pre-curated or determined ahead of time through a guide book or atelier master. Rather, for Brunelleschi, the struggles and strangeness of living abroad were linked intimately with the task of discovering architecture. This duality promotes a vision of study abroad that is not based on canonical learning but rather on becoming an architect through challenging one's cultural boundaries, inventing solutions amidst uncertainty, and taking command of one's personal curiosities.

It becomes quite entertaining, then, to link some of Brunelleschi's activities with a few of the anecdotes of this book, itself emitted from the city where Filippo called home. For instance, in recording and inventing ways to record one's surroundings, we can easily refer back to chapter five (BYOSB! Bring your own sketchbook), on the importance of learning to sketch, or chapter seven (Steal! And then return like the bees do), on how studying great buildings or ideas of the past forges a path toward the re-invention of those ideas in new ways. I also am reminded in chapters nine (Fall in love!) and thirteen (Get your hands D] dirty!) of how Brunelleschi eschewed the pleasures of eating and sleeping and singularly focused on architecture while in Roma, using his physical and mental resourcefulness to excavate knowledge and new ideas wherever they could be found. And finally, when following the advice in chapter sixteen (How tall is a chair in centimeters?) to a carry a metric ruler and measure common objects, Brunelleschi's obsessions with first-hand knowledge of measures and proportions comes to mind. The astute reader will no doubt find many other connections between Brunelleschi's journey and the opportunities for an architecture student to study abroad today.

Although Brunelleschi arrived to measure the monuments, they were not tourist attractions like today. He literally had to excavate the city to find them. Quite apart from "bagging" his findings, Filippo had to take tools out of his bag and actively engage with his context. Today, with the monuments on full display, framed by guidebooks and regulated by ticket sales, the discerning student can re-live Brunelleschi's journey not by focusing on the great buildings of the past but by doing their own digging. Your tools: a sketchbook, an open mind, and the tenacity to follow your measuring stick and shovel, wherever it may take you.

Printed in China by ORO Editions
2021